Recognising and Planning for Special Needs in the Early Years

Chris Dukes and Maggie Smith

SAGE

Los Angeles | London | New Delhi
Singapore | Washington DC

First published 2009

SAGE Publications Ltd
1 Oliver's Yard
55 City Road
London EC1Y 1SP

SAGE Publications Inc.
2455 Teller Road
Thousand Oaks, California 91320

SAGE Publications India Pvt Ltd
B 1/I 1 Mohan Cooperative Industrial Area
Mathura Road
New Delhi 110 044

SAGE Publications Asia-Pacific Pte Ltd
33 Pekin Street #02-01
Far East Square
Singapore 048763

Library of Congress Control Number: 2008934332

British Library Cataloguing in Publication data

A catalogue record for this book is available from the British Library

ISBN 978-1-84787-521-1
ISBN 978-1-84787-522-8(pbk)

Typeset by C&M Digitals (P) Ltd, Chennai, India
Printed in India by Replika Press Pvt. Ltd.
Printed on paper from sustainable resources

Recognising and Planning for
Special Needs in the Early Years

Hands On Guide Series

Written by two Area SENCOs who work closely with pre-school SENCOs and managers on a daily basis, these books are packed with ready-to-use activities, photocopiable worksheets and advice ideal for all those working with the 0 to 5 age range, such as pre-school practitioners, nursery managers, advisory teachers, SENCOs, inclusion officers and child care and education students and tutors.

Other books in the series are:

A Practical Guide to Pre-School Inclusion (2006)

Developing Pre-School Communication and Language (2007)

Working with Parents of Children with Special Educational Needs (2007)

Building Better Behaviour in the Early Years (2009)

Contents

About the authors

Chris Dukes is a qualified teacher with over 20 years' experience. She has worked in various London primary schools as a class teacher and later as a member of the Senior Management Team. Chris has a Masters degree in Special Needs and through her later roles as a SENCO and support teacher, many years' experience of working with children with a variety of needs. Chris has worked closely with staff teams, mentoring, advising and supervising work with children with additional needs, as well as with other education and health professionals. Chris currently works as an Area SENCO supporting Special Needs Coordinators and managers in a wide range of pre-school settings. As well as advising she writes courses, delivers training and produces publications.

Maggie Smith began her career as a nursery teacher in Birmingham. She has worked as a peripatetic teacher for an under-5s EAL Team and went on to become the Foundation Stage manager of an Early Years Unit in Inner London. Maggie helped to set up an innovative unit for young children with behavioural difficulties and has also worked supporting families of children with special needs. She has taught on Early Years BTEC and CACHE courses at a college of higher education. She currently works as an Area SENCO supporting Special Needs Coordinators and managers in a wide range of pre-school settings. As well as advising she writes courses, delivers training and produces publications.

Acknowledgements

This book is dedicated to all the practitioners, children and parents we have had the privilege of working with and learning from.

Contents of the CD-ROM

How to use the CD-ROM

The CD-ROM contains pdf files of the worksheets from this book organised by chapter. You will need Acrobat Reader version 3 or higher to view and print these pages.

The documents are set to print at A4 but you can enlarge them to A3 by increasing the output percentage using the page set-up settings for your printer.

Throughout the book, you will see this CD icon used ●. This indicates that the material you are looking at is also available electronically on the accompanying CD-ROM.

Contents of the CD-ROM

Introduction

Chapter 5

Chapter 6

Chapter 7

Chapter 8

Introduction

Our starting point for writing this book is illustrated by the following scenario. It is a situation in which many practioners often find themselves.

It is the end of the day at Wonderland Nursery. Kath and Hollie are tidying up the room ready for the next day. The following conversation takes place.

Kath: 'I'm a bit worried about Johnny.'

Hollie: 'Why, what's the matter?'

Kath: 'I don't know really, I can't put my finger on it but I feel that something's not quite right.'

Hollie: 'I know what you mean. Maybe you should have a word with his Mum.'

Kath: 'I would but I don't want to worry her, especially if it turns out to be nothing.'

Hollie: 'Have you spoken to Sheila? She's an experienced manager, she'll probably know what to do.'

Kath: 'Well I did mention it to her, she didn't really say much. Mind you I was a bit vague; I just said I was a bit concerned about him!'

Hollie: 'Can you narrow it down to a particular area of his development that you are worried about?'

Kath: 'I think it's mainly his language. He doesn't really seem to be saying much and he hardly ever plays with the other children. He usually walks away when they go anywhere near him.'

Hollie: 'Why don't you try doing some themed observations – that usually helps. I'll look at them with you, if you'd like.'

Kath: 'Good idea. I don't know why I didn't think of doing some before. I'll have a look at a child development book as well.'

Hollie: 'That new book Sheila's just bought is really good. It gives you child development information so that you can compare it with the child you have in mind. It links everything to the EYFS and it gives you a step-by-step guide on what to do if you're still worried.'

Kath: 'Great, I'd better go and find it! What's it called again … ?'

We hope that by writing this book practitioners will be provided with the support they need to help young children and their parents move forward in a positive way.

One of the most exciting things when working with young children is that as practitioners we are constantly learning new things and having our ideas challenged. Every child we meet will teach us something new and change the way we think about their learning. None more so than

a child who has or may have an additional need. We don't need to be experts but we do need to have an open mind, a willingness to be flexible and adaptable and to believe that we have something to offer every child.

A 'can do' approach is the single most important requirement for inclusion and the biggest barrier to including all children is not accessibility, resources or equipment but individual attitudes. Just as we see each child as an individual we must also see each practitioner as an individual. This is why reflective practice is so important. It gives us the opportunity to analyse not only our practice but also the thoughts, ideas and perceptions which underpin this practice.

Many practitioners are either reluctant or feel they do not have the skills to identify any additional needs of children in their care. This could be for many reasons including fear of approaching parents, fear of labelling children or fear of getting it wrong.

However, a practitioner's role is not to diagnose but to observe and identify where a child may be experiencing difficulties. Strategies can then be put in place to support the child and, if concerns still remain after a period of time, to make an appropriate referral to a specialist.

Practitioners would rarely do this without support from local authority advisors such as Area SENCOs or advisory teachers.

Chapter 1 sets the scene and lays out the legal and advisory framework within which all early years providers work. It places the early identification of additional needs firmly within those frameworks.

Chapters 2 – 8 follow the outline of a Five-step guide to recognising and planning for additional needs. This will demystify the process and guide you through the various stages from gathering initial information to writing an individual education plan.

Pre-school practitioners

This book will enable you to identify children with special needs in your pre-school setting. You will be supported by practical examples, developmental guidance and formats to use within your setting. These can be used as presented in the book or adapted or personalised to suit your own needs. The Hands-on activities will provide a starting point for team discussion.

Tutors and students

Through reading this book you will increase your awareness of the steps needed to identify children's special needs. It will give you clear guidance on how to incorporate these steps into everyday practice and planning. The Hands-on Activities can be used as short assignments.

Advisers

Use this book to support pre-schools to improve their knowledge, understanding and practice for identifying special needs. Stand-alone chapters can be used as a basis for training.

A note on the text

The case studies included in this publication are composites of numerous children in various settings, distilled from the authors' many years of experience. They are not specific to any one child-practitioner or setting.

Five Steps to Recognising Additional Needs

Step 1

A Unique Child – A Holistic View
Think about what you already know.
Think about what is happening in the child's life and family circumstances.
Talk to parents.

Step 2

Enabling Environments – The Reflective Setting
Reflect upon your own setting and practice.
What is the child's experience of a day in your nursery?
Are you differentiating and adapting to meet their needs?
Talk to staff.

Step 3

Development Matters
Think about what might be developmentally appropriate for the child.
Consider their age and stage of development.
Remember every child will develop at a different pace, in different areas, at different times.

Step 4

Look, Listen and Note
Focus on the child's areas of strength and those which are causing concern.
Carry out three or four targeted observations in the area of difficulty.
Try to have more than one person doing the observations.
Analyse your observations using the appropriate follow-up sheet.
What are the most important points you have noted?

Step 5

Plan, Do, Review
Decide on a plan of action.
How can you use the child's strengths?
What needs to be done and who is going to do it?
Review your plan and monitor progress.
If there are still concerns after several reviews, with parental permission, seek further advice.

 Recognising and Planning for Special Needs in the Early Years, SAGE © Chris Dukes and Maggie Smith, 2009

CHAPTER ONE

The bigger picture: the law, guidance and recommendations

Practitioners are encouraged to **'identify and respond early to needs which could lead to the development of learning difficulties'** (EYFS Practice Guidance, page 6, para 1.10).

In order to support practitioners to fulfil the above responsibility, this chapter aims to outline the various legal requirements, guidance and recommendations which govern early years practice. It also highlights the references within the documentation which relate to the early recognition of additional needs.

In so doing we hope to show that the process of recognising additional needs is not only the province of specialists but is the collective responsibility of all practitioners. The tools and systems needed to identify those children who may have additional needs are already woven into the fabric of every setting. The starting point should be practitioners looking at each child holistically as an individual and striving to meet their needs in order for them to reach their potential – a theme which runs through all current thinking about early education.

The chapter sets out guidance on:

▶ government policy

▶ the Early Years Foundation Stage

▶ the Special Educational Needs Code of Practice

▶ the Disability Discrimination Act.

An overview

The government has made it policy over the past few years to create good quality, affordable child care and education for all children.

At the heart of this policy lies **_Every Child Matters_**, a document which identifies five outcomes for children that should be achieved no matter where they live, whatever their needs or the services they use. It sets down the basic principle that it is the duty of all those caring for and working with children to ensure that their needs are identified and met.

The five outcomes are to:

▶ stay safe

▶ be healthy

▶ enjoy and achieve

▶ achieve economic well-being

▶ make a positive contribution.

The government's ten-year strategy for childcare, **Choice for Parents, the Best Start for Children**, promised to establish a single coherent development and learning framework for all young children from birth to the age of five.

From September 2008 the **Early Years Foundation Stage (EYFS)** is the relevant framework. The ultimate aim of the framework is to help children achieve all five of the *Every Child Matters* outcomes.

The government also recently formed the National Strategies SEN/LDD Programme and Adviser Team. One of the roles of this team is to advise local authorities on the implementation and development of their SEN policies, provision and practice. The aim is to help local authorities and schools to narrow the gap in achievement for groups of vulnerable children and to improve the links between SEN programmes and national strategies, including the EYFS.

Another key government SEN strategy document **Removing Barriers to Achievement** also originally proposed the **Inclusion Development Programme (IDP)** which was finally launched in October 2007. The IDP aims to support schools and early years settings by helping them develop more inclusive practice and to raise awareness and confidence among staff about dealing with various kinds of SEN.

This is to be done through a yearly focus on a particular aspect of special needs. Training and materials will be developed by the National Strategies Team alongside voluntary and specialist organisations and then disseminated to the various phases of education, including early years.

All practitioners should therefore have access to further training in various aspects of special needs.

The Early Years Foundation Stage

The guiding principles of the EYFS place each individual child at the centre of care and the curriculum. It stresses the importance of looking at children holistically and the duty of all practitioners to meet their often diverse needs.

> *The EYFS framework is designed to be fully inclusive of all children's needs, recognising the need to respond to differences of ethnicity, culture, religion or belief, home language, family background, SEN, disability, gender or ability. There is significant flexibility to provide the six areas of learning and development in a way that reflects the needs and circumstances of each child.*

(EYFS Statutory Framework, page 41, para 4.3)

Section 2 of the **Statutory Framework** details the learning and development requirements. It outlines the educational programmes to be taught to young children, the early learning goals and the assessment arrangements for their achievements.

Section 3 of the **Statutory Framework** details the welfare requirements. Throughout these requirements there are references to meeting the individual needs of children at an appropriate level.

Under the ***equal opportunities*** section there is a specific legal requirement for all providers to:

> have and implement an effective policy about ensuring equality of opportunities and for supporting children with learning difficulties and disabilities.

Also mentioned here is that all providers should 'have regard to' the Special Educational Needs Code of Practice (DfEE, 2001).

The statutory guidance referred to should be incorporated into a policy on ***equality of opportunities*** and should include the following:

- information about how the individual needs of all children will be met;
- information about how all children, including those who are disabled or have special educational needs, will be included, valued and supported, and how reasonable adjustments will be made for them;
- a commitment to working with parents and other agencies;
- information about how the SEN Code of Practice is put into practice in the provision;
- the name of the Special Educational Needs Coordinator;
- arrangements for reviewing, monitoring and evaluating the effectiveness of inclusive practices;
- information about how the provision will promote and value diversity and differences;
- information about how inappropriate attitudes and practices will be challenged;
- information about how the provision will encourage children to value and respect others.

The accompanying ***Practice Guidance for the EYFS*** also stresses that the principles and policies should be reflected in practice.

Practitioners must *promote positive attitudes to diversity and difference within all children* (page 6, para. 1.8).

Practitioners must also *plan for the needs of any children with learning difficulties or disabilities* (page 6, para. 1.9)

With a focus on removing or helping to counter underachievement and overcoming barriers for children where these already exist, practitioners should also identify and respond early to needs which could lead to the development of learning difficulties (page 6, para. 1.10).

The **Principles into Practice,** cards divide the principles into four key ***themes***:

- **A Unique Child**
- **Positive Relationships**

▶ **Enabling Environments**

▶ **Learning and Development.**

Each of these themes is then supported by commitments which describe how these inclusive principles can be put into practice. For example, the theme of 'A Unique Child states:

> Every child is a competent learner from birth who can be resilient, capable, confident and self-assured.

It is recognised that babies and children develop in individual ways and at varying rates (Principles into Practice card 1.1). Practitioners are urged to:

> Identity the need for additional support as early as possible

and it is pointed out that:

> Knowing when and how to call in specialist help is one important element of inclusive practice. (Principles into Practice card 1.2)

Hands-on activity

Look at the EYFS Principles into Practice cards and find further references to identifying and planning for individual needs, e.g.

'Enabling environments' card 3.1.

▶ 'babies and children are individuals first, each with a unique profile of abilities …'

▶

The Special Educational Needs Code of Practice (DfEE, 2001)

The early identification of learning difficulties and disabilities is key in current thinking. This is also stressed in the SEN Code of Practice (2001) which has already been established as important guidance and which runs alongside the EYFS.

The Code of Practice outlines certain expectations with regard to identifying and meeting the needs of children with learning difficulties and/or disabilities. These include a series of principles that early years settings are expected to adhere to.

The principles of the Code of Practice

▸ Every child with special educational needs should have their needs met.

▸ As far as possible these needs will be met within a mainstream setting with access to a broad, balanced and relevant curriculum.

▸ The views of parents should be sought and taken into account.

▸ Wherever possible the views of the child should be taken into account.

(DfEE, 2001, page 16, para. 2.2).

What do we mean by special educational needs?

The legal definition of SEN (Education Act 1996) as set out in the Code of Practice (DfEE, 2001) is:

> *Children have special educational needs if they have a learning difficulty which calls for special educational provision to be made for them.*
>
> *Children have a learning difficulty if they:*
>
> (a) *have a significantly greater difficulty than the majority of children of the same age;*
>
> *or*
>
> (b) *have a disability which prevents or hinders them from making use of the educational facilities to be found locally for children of the same age;*
>
> (c) *are under compulsory school age and fall within the definition at (a) or (b) above or would do so if special educational provision was not made for them.*

The Code of Practice describes **special educational needs** as falling into four main areas:

▶ Communication and interaction

▶ Cognition and learning

▶ Behavioural, emotional and social development

▶ Sensory and physical.

Some children of course will have difficulties in more than one of these areas.

Roles and responsibilities

The Code of Practice assigns the day-to-day organisation and coordination of special needs provision to the Special Educational Needs Coordinator (SENCO). However, it also clearly states that identification of, planning for and working with children with special needs, learning difficulties and disabilities lies firmly with *all* members of staff.

Policies and procedures

The Code of Practice sets out very clearly the procedures to be followed once a child is identified as having special or additional needs. The importance of both parental involvement and child participation is a key principle in this process.

The actions which follow are called a *graduated response* whic1h is further explained in Chapter 8.

The Disability Discrimination Act 1995

A large group of children currently attending our pre-school settings are covered by the duties of the Disability Discrimination Act 1995 (DDA).

The DDA sets out two *core duties*:

> 1. Not to treat a disabled child less favourably.
> 2. To make reasonable adjustments for disabled children.
>
> From October 2004 '*reasonable adjustments*' include removing physical barriers.
>
> The core duties are **anticipatory** and provision and plans for disabled children should therefore be in place before they might actually be needed.

The DDA has implications for all aspects of early years settings policies' and practice and also sits well alongside the principles of the EYFS.

The idea that settings need to include in their equal opportunities policies information about how reasonable adjustments will be made to cater for individual needs has already been mentioned. The anticipatory nature of these duties also means that settings will need to be aware of what might be needed and plan for future eventualities.

Further reading

Department for Education and Employment (2001) *Special Educational Needs: Code of Practice*: DfEE

Department for Education and Skills (2007) *Statutory Framework for the Early Years Foundation Stage*. DfES.

Department for Education and Skills (2008) *Practice Guidance for the Early Years Foundation Stage*. DfES.

National Children's Bureau Enterprise Ltd (2003) *Early Years and the Disability Discrimination Act 1995: What Service Providers Need to Know*. NCB.

CHAPTER TWO

A unique child: a holistic view

The aim of this chapter is to show that there are many factors to be considered before any conclusions can be reached about the needs a child may have.

When practitioners or carers are concerned about a child's progress or development it is all too easy to immediately think about the child only in terms of the perceived difficulty and what might be 'their problem'. A far better approach is to take a holistic view of the child.

This chapter sets out:

▶ thinking about what you already know about the child

▶ factors which can affect a child's learning and development

▶ talking to parents

and includes:

▶ case studies

▶ a Hands-on activity

▶ Further reading.

Think about what you already know

A good place to begin if you have any concerns about a child is to gather information. Most practitioners know more than they think they do about individual children. Often it is only when you start to focus and really gather all the different pieces of information together that you begin to see the whole child.

▶ Consider what you already know about a particular child – their personality, likes, dislikes, preferred learning style, etc.

▶ Talk to colleagues who may have a different view or perspective.

▶ Look at any written information such as your admissions form, previous reports, etc.

▶ Think about the child's strengths and areas which have improved or are developing well.

▶ Consider whether your concerns are new or whether you have always had them.

Think about what is happening in the child's life and family circumstances

There are many factors which can affect a child in the short term and for longer periods of time. These factors are mostly beyond your control but as practitioners you often have to deal with the consequences and effects on the child.

Some of the factors centre on physical needs such as lack of sleep, illness or poor living conditions. Some are connected to family circumstances such as bereavement or separation while others have their roots in change. Like adults many children find change quite difficult, whether it is moving into a new bedroom, a new house or having a new routine or carer.

While each child will react differently to a given set of circumstances, these factors can result in children displaying a whole range of needs. Practitioners may notice a change in a child's behaviour, concentration, attitude, emotional state or rate of progress.

The diagram on page 9 illustrates some of the factors which can contribute to a child needing some extra support for a period of time.

Talk to parents or carers

Parents are children first and most enduring educators. When parents and practitioners work together in early years settings, the results have a positive impact on children's development and learning.

(EYFS Principles into Practice card 2.2)

Mutual respect, a valuing of diversity and effective communication are essential to forming good relationships with parents. These are particularly important when practitioners have to discuss more difficult issues or concerns about a child.

Any meeting should be regarded as a two-way exchange of information, with the possibility of both partners learning from each other. Discussions with parents can give practitioners insights into a child's personality, feelings or interests outside of the pre-school, and because parents spend time with their child in varying situations these can reveal a different side to a child's nature.

It is very important that when you talk to a child's parents or carers about any concerns you may have that you are open-minded and non-judgemental. All concerns should be handled sensitively and in a way that will not cause alarm or appear as prying into their family life.

Factors Which Can Affect a Child's Progress or Behaviour

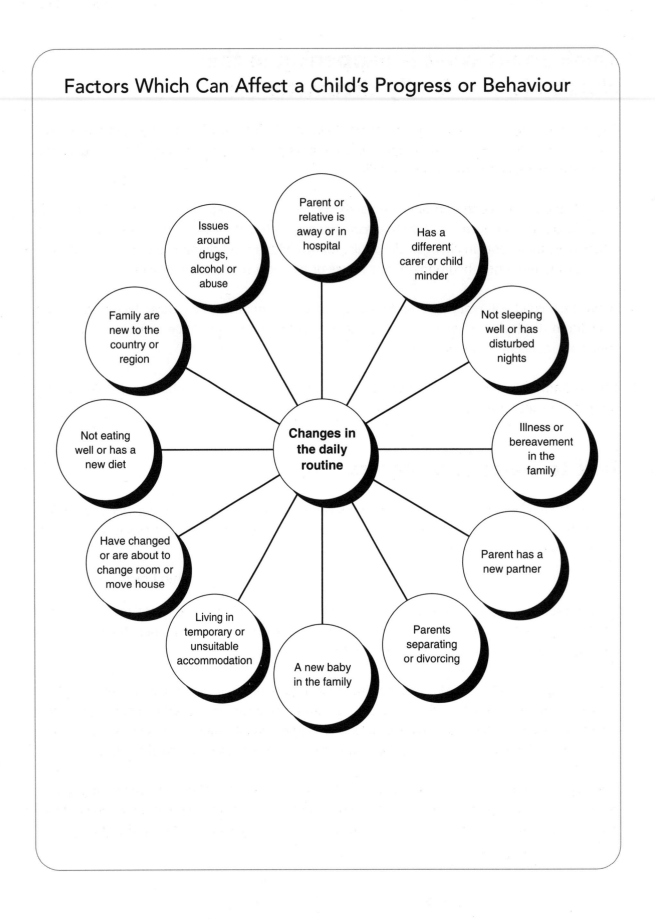

Communicating with parents

Careful thought and preparation should go into any meeting, particularly the timing and arrangements for a private place to talk. It is also essential to have a method of recording meetings with parents. Notes can be taken at the time and copies given to all involved.

This ensures that practitioners and parents have a clear reminder of what was discussed and what was agreed at the meeting.

Sometimes a meeting can reveal that there have been changes in a child's life which parents may not have shared with you because they did not feel that they were important. While on the surface these might seem insignificant they can upset a child enough to make a difference to their behaviour, progress or development.

At other times there are changes which parents have not shared because they are very personal. It is very important therefore to make it clear why you are asking particular questions, that you are interested in factors which are affecting the child, and who you will be sharing the information with.

It is very helpful if you already have a routine method of keeping in touch with parents. Many settings have systems for meeting with parents regularly in the form of either pastoral or general progress meetings. Others have communication books or diaries which go back and forth between home and setting. Parents as well as practitioners can contribute to observations and records which keep both informed of a child's latest developments.

Often the process of gathering information provides enough evidence for you to plan how you might support the child in their current situation, as illustrated by the following case studies.

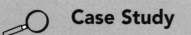 **Case Study**

Alice

Alice is three years old and has been at the nursery for a term. She settled quite quickly and mum usually dropped her off in the morning.

Mum had a new baby girl in the Christmas holidays. Since the beginning of the new term Alice has been reluctant to come to nursery and cries when her father, who now drops her off in the morning, leaves. Alice is starting to have tantrums at nursery when she can't do what she wants to and is often observed snatching toys away from other children.

Alice's key person decided to share her concerns with the setting's special needs/inclusion coordinator, whose advice was first to gather more information about Alice.

What we already know

Since Alice started at nursery:

- before this term Alice was very settled at nursery.

- Alice has always been kind to other children.

- Alice enjoys playing in the home corner with her friend Louise.

- Alice loves sharing books.

There have been some changes in Alice's life recently which she may be having difficulty adjusting to:

- Alice has a new baby sister.

- dad is dropping her off instead of mum.

Information from Alice's key person:

- Karen, Alice's key person, has noticed that Alice becomes tearful very quickly.

- Most of the incidents with other children happen just before lunch time when Alice seems tired and grumpy.

Karen decides to arrange a meeting with Alice's father, Mr Jones. She quietly takes him to one side and asks when a convenient time to have a chat would be. He has a few days off during the following week so an appointment is made and Karen arranges for the setting manager to cover her while she talks to Mr Jones.

At the end of the meeting Karen has a plan for the nursery and parents to support Alice. Another meeting is arranged for six weeks later to review progress.

Sample Record of Meeting with Parents 1

Record of meeting with parents	Date: 10 January 2008
Child's name: Alice Jones **Present at meeting:** Karen (key person)	**D.o.B.** 10-10-04 Mr Jones (father)

Reason for the meeting:

Concern about Alice being distressed in the mornings and about changes in her behaviour.

Information/what was discussed:

Alice's dad reports that Alice was very excited about having a new baby sister.

It has been very busy at home over the holiday with lots of visitors calling to see the new baby.

Alice has had quite a few late nights because of various family events and parties and has not got back into her usual bedtime routine.

Alice has become quite tearful at home and parents feel that she may be jealous of all the attention that the new baby is receiving.

Alice has complained that she wants mummy to take her to nursery but her mother is not getting much sleep and has not been well.

For the time being dad will be dropping Alice at nursery but he is not able to stay very long to settle her because he has to catch the train to work.

Alice's grandmother who she usually spends a lot of time with has been on holiday for two weeks but is due back in a couple of days.

What should happen next:

Karen will read some stories about new baby brothers and sisters to the whole group so that Alice has a chance to acknowledge some of her feelings.

Karen will turn the home corner into a baby clinic and invite one of the mothers who Is a midwife to talk to the children about looking after babies.

Karen will make sure that a communication book is set up to keep Alice's mum informed about what Alice has done at nursery, so that she can talk about it at home.

Alice's parents will try to involve Alice more with the baby and make sure that she has some 1:1 time each evening with mum.

Parents will try to get Alice's bedtime routine back to normal.

Parents will ask Grandma to bring Alice to nursery as she will have more time to go through the settling in process again with Alice if necessary.

The situation will be reviewed in six weeks' time.

Signed: K. Tucker **(setting)**	**Signed:** C. Jones **(parent)**

Recognising and Planning for Special Needs in the Early Years, SAGE © Chris Dukes and Maggie Smith

Sample Record of Meeting with Parents 2

Record of meeting with parents	Date: 24 February 2008
Child's name: Alice Jones **Present at meeting:** Karen (key person)	**D.o.B.** 10-10-04 Mr Jones and Mrs Jones (parents)

Reason for the meeting:

Review of Alice's progress

Information/what was discussed:

Karen had been giving Alice some extra attention and has carried out the ideas on the action plan.

Alice had loved the baby clinic and was very proud to show off her knowledge about babies when the midwife came to give her talk.

The whole group had enjoyed stories about the arrival of new baby brothers and sisters, In fact this helped another child whose mother is expecting a baby in a couple of months' time.

The communication book had worked really well and Alice loved her mum reading the messages about what she had been doing. Karen had also sent some photos home.

The incidents involving other children had decreased dramatically and Alice did not seem as tired.

Parents had managed to get Alice back into her bedtime routine by making this her 'special time' with mum.

Alice was also helping to bath and put the baby to bed.

Alice's grandma dropped her off at nursery for about a month and although it seemed like a backwards step at first, having another gradual settling in period had reduced Alice's distress at being left.

Mrs Jones and baby sister Heather had been bringing Alice to nursery for the past two weeks and had got into a good morning routine. After an initial 'wobble' Alice was now happy to be left.

What should happen next:

Staff will continue to keep an eye on Alice to make sure the progress continues.

Mrs. Jones will be bringing Heather in to the nursery when she comes to tell groups of children stories as part of book week.

No further action is needed at the moment.

Signed: K. Tucker **(setting)**	Signed: C. Jones **(parent)**

 Recognising and Planning for Special Needs in the Early Years, SAGE © Chris Dukes and Maggie Smith, 2009

Case Study

Mtumba

Mtumba has recently joined the nursery. Her family has recently arrived in Britain and are seeking asylum. The family are living in temporary accommodation and have a bus journey to bring Mtumba to pre-school; they have another child to get to a nearby school as well as a six-month-old baby. Her mother speaks no English but her father speaks a little.

Mtumba spends most of the time wandering around the nursery or watching other children from a distance. She makes very little eye contact and does not respond in any way when spoken to. She is very reluctant to go outside and if staff try to encourage her she will often scream and run away. At snack time she appears to be very hungry but refuses to sit at the snack table.

Factors which may be affecting Mtumba:

- The language, climate and environment are new, different and unfamiliar.

- She may have lost her home, relatives, friends or belongings.

- She has possibly been frightened, in danger or have witnessed violence.

- She may be suffering from bereavement.

- Her parents and family may be stressed, distressed or unhappy.

- She may not have seen or had experience of the equipment and activities of the pre-school.

- She may feel insecure or vulnerable, particularly outside.

- She may not have eaten before she comes to pre-school.

- She may be worried about what she can eat or about sharing food for religious or cultural reasons.

Things to try:

- Meet with Mtumba's parents – seek help from local community groups or other parents who can translate.

- Find out as much as possible about the family history but remember there can be very sensitive issues which need careful handling.

- Offer her a snack when she comes to pre-school – ask parents about her eating routines at home.

- Allow extra time for Mtumba to get used to the pre-school with plenty of opportunities to watch and observe.

▶ Encourage her to join in with activities at her own pace and level, if and when she is ready.

▶ Model the use of toys and equipment and encourage other children to do so.

▶ Consider sending some toys and books home for Mtumba to play with.

▶ Help her to understand the routines of the pre-school by making a book of photographs. This can be taken home to share with parents.

▶ Use gesture and signs as well as simple language when communicating with her. Do not initially expect a response.

▶ Try to find an activity that Mtumba enjoys and gradually move it towards the outside area.

▶ Time outside on her own with an adult and one or two other children may feel less threatening.

As these case studies illustrate, the process of gathering information and talking to parents and other practitioners often provides us with a much clearer picture of what a child's needs may be.

By considering the child as a whole, their strengths, personality, background and circumstances, and by talking to those who know them best, ideas of how the child can best be supported often become apparent and can easily be planned for.

For many children this process is enough to help them move forward and although progress should be reviewed and monitored no further intervention may be required.

For other children it may be necessary to move on to the next step in seeking to identify what or if they have additional needs.

Hands-on activity

Consider how you could improve or implement a system for keeping in touch with parents in your setting, including those who have English as an additional language, e.g.

▶ text messages.

▶

Think about and discuss with other staff how issues of confidentiality are dealt with in your setting.

Further reading

Dukes, Chris and Smith, Maggie (2007) *Working with Parents of Children with Special Educational Needs*, Hands On Guides. Paul Chapman Publishing.
See the website of the National Refugee Integration Forum (www.nrif.org.uk) for advice on how to support young refugee children and their parents.

CHAPTER THREE

Enabling environments: the reflective setting

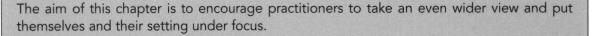

> The aim of this chapter is to encourage practitioners to take an even wider view and put themselves and their setting under focus.
>
> Being reflective is the cornerstone of good early years practice. Taking a longer-term view of change and recognising that there is always more to learn is a common feature of many outstanding settings.
>
> The following pages will support whole staff teams and managers to reflect upon how the environment they have created may affect a young child's progress and improve the inclusiveness of the setting as a whole.
>
> This chapter sets out:
>
> ◗ how to reflect upon your own setting and practice
>
> ◗ factors to consider when thinking about your setting
>
> and includes:
>
> ◗ case studies to illustrate the reflective process
>
> ◗ a Hands-on activity
>
> ◗ further reading.

A starting point

When practitioners have concerns about a child's progress, as we have said in Chapter 2, the best practice is to take a wider view of the child and begin to look holistically at factors in a child's life that may be relevant.

We know that young children can be and are affected by everything around them so practitioners should be aware of how their setting's routines and practices affect each child. A good place for practitioners to begin to reflect is by asking some simple questions such as:

◗ What is a child's experience of a day in your nursery?

◗ Are you differentiating and adapting to meet their needs?

◗ Is the child's experience in your setting contributing to or even causing difficulties?

Organisation, atmosphere and routines provide the foundation of any pre-school establishment. This is the very thing that parents have responded positively to when they chose to send their child to your setting. First impressions are always important but often things are not as straight-forward as they seem.

The everyday management of a setting needs skill and expertise. Management issues can include staff sickness and holidays, or it may be difficult to find time for training, and sometimes individual practitioners may not have ideal working relationships. The reasons are many and varied and are familiar to all managers.

Individual managers have first and foremost to balance the needs of the children alongside those of their parents and staff.

Reflective practice

Beginning to reflect upon some examples of your setting's routines and daily practice

Good practitioners are by definition reflective practitioners – they strive for progression of their practice, they challenge and question themselves and they look for new and better ways of working. They do all of this for one reason – to improve the opportunities for learning for the children in their care.

Once practitioners get into the habit of regularly reflecting upon their own practice and their own setting's routines obvious pitfalls can begin to be avoided. Practitioners can then be secure in the knowledge that they are not contributing to any difficulties a child may encounter with their learning.

The diagram on page 21 outlines some circumstances that practitioners may consider for reflection while the case studies below are examples of how the routines and practice of a busy setting may adversely affect a child's progress. The descriptions outlined are not exhaustive but they bring to attention common cases which, although not immediately obvious, *do* exacerbate some children's difficulties.

Involving children in their own learning

Just as setting staff are developing their reflective practice so too should we encourage children to reflect and make choices about their own learning. Children who feel part of the nursery community usually exhibit a high quality of learning. They often display positive behaviours, empathy with their peers and a genuine enthusiasm for knowledge.

On reflection

Questions to support reflection

▶ Do the children in your setting have access to a wide variety of self-selected activities and equipment?

▶ Are the children encouraged to make choices about what they want to do and achieve?

▶ Are children taught how to be reflective about their learning and behaviour?

▶ Are children given the time and space to complete their activities to a level they are satisfied with?

Possible solutions

Staff could be encouraged to give children *choices* about what they are going to do. They can make equipment and resources available to children to self-select and they can support children to develop a ***plan, do, review*** approach. For example:

▶ 'What are you going to do?'

▶ 'Can I help you?'

Reflecting on Setting and Practice

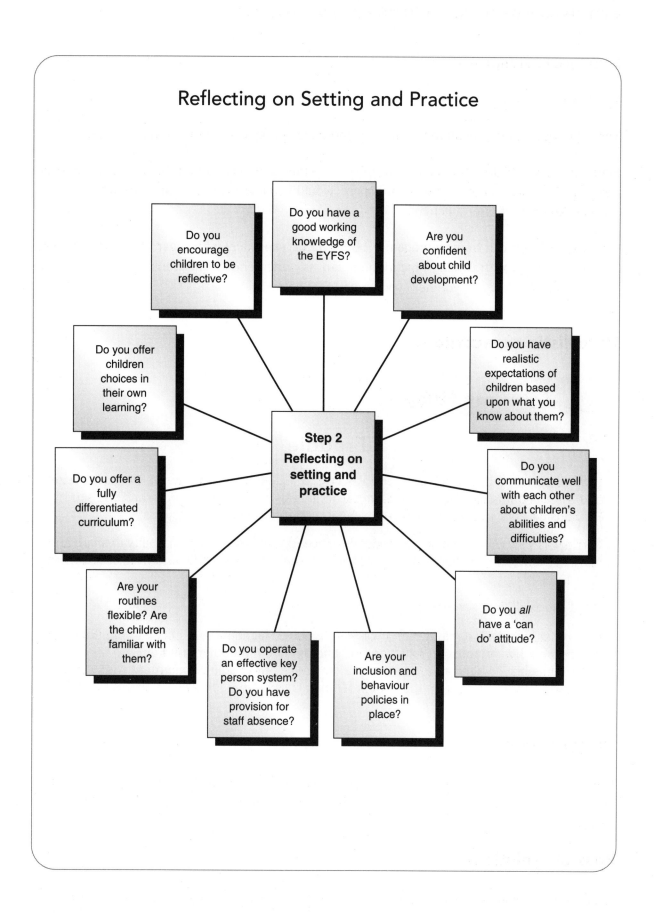

Do you encourage children to be reflective?

Do you have a good working knowledge of the EYFS?

Are you confident about child development?

Do you offer children choices in their own learning?

Do you have realistic expectations of children based upon what you know about them?

Step 2
Reflecting on setting and practice

Do you offer a fully differentiated curriculum?

Do you communicate well with each other about children's abilities and difficulties?

Are your routines flexible? Are the children familiar with them?

Do you operate an effective key person system? Do you have provision for staff absence?

Are your inclusion and behaviour policies in place?

Do you *all* have a 'can do' attitude?

▶ 'Do you need anything?'

▶ 'How did your activity go?'

Through observation practitioners can learn how to support children with their choices.

Staff could give children the *time* to complete activities and play without being rushed onto the next thing, e.g. *less* 'time to tidy up' *and more* 'would you like me to put this somewhere safe so you can finish it off after lunch?'

Similarly children can be encouraged to be *reflective*, especially with regard to their behaviour and relationships with others. Practitioners can ask open-ended questions, e.g. 'How do you think he feels?' 'How can you help your friend feel better?'

Unrealistic expectations

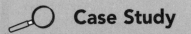 **Case Study**

Freddie

Freddie attends a day-care setting from 8 a.m. to 4 p.m. five days a week. He is two years and three months old. His key person Carrie is new to the toddler room and the setting. Previously Carrie worked in a nursery school with three and four year olds.

Carrie was very concerned about Freddie's concentration abilities, his inability to share and his short temper. She shared her concerns with the setting SENCO who in turn observed Freddie.

What the SENCO observed:

▶ Freddie sat for five minutes and was very involved listening to a story for that time. For the next five minutes he rolled around and annoyed the other children.
▶ Freddie played alongside his peers but was reluctant to share equipment with them.
▶ Freddie threw himself on the floor when he couldn't immediately get access to a bike.

On reflection

The SENCO felt that all the above was appropriate for a child of Freddie's age. The SENCO realised that some of the expectations held by the room staff – and Carrie in particular – were unrealistic.

Possible solutions

▶ Story time could be made shorter so as not to last longer than five minutes and perhaps the groups could be smaller.

▶ Freddie could participate in sharing and turn-taking activities with staff to get him used to the idea of sharing.

▶ Room staff could use a sand timer to ensure that all children get equal access to the bikes. This would be explained and modelled to *all* of the children.

▶ The SENCO could arrange training for all staff on the **Practice Guidance for the Early Years Foundation Stage**.

▶ The setting could invest in some early years guides and child development books for staff to refer to.

▶ Senior staff could be encouraged to involve themselves much more in the day-to-day planning of the setting.

Inflexible routines

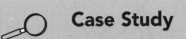

Case Study

Haroon

Haroon's behaviour was worrying all the staff. He was angry and aggressive towards staff and the other children. Through observation staff found out that Haroon's difficulties were especially evident first thing in the morning. By mid-morning his mood had usually altered and he seemed like a different child.

On reflection

Staff, as well as observing Haroon, looked at their own routines during that busy time of the session. They had a system in place where all the children shared a snack at 10 o'clock and they realised that Haroon's behaviour improved after snack time. Haroon usually arrived at the setting at 8 a.m.

A possible solution

Staff changed their snack time routine so that the children could have access to breakfast as soon as they arrived or when they wanted it.

Haroon got into the habit of having something to eat as soon as he arrived and his behaviour improved markedly.

Key person

A key person has special responsibilities for working with a small number of children, giving them the reassurance to feel safe and cared for and building relationships with their parents.

(EYFS Practice Guidance, page 15, para. 3.4)

Case Study

Farhana

Farhana attends a children's centre and is three years old. She has been at the centre for over a year and is well settled. Her progress has been good. Lately, however, Farhana has been unsettled. She is clingy with her parents in the mornings and has started to be non-cooperative with setting staff. Previously at small group time Farhana loved to participate, joining in with role-play and singing songs. Staff now report that she is difficult to manage and has on several occasions disrupted the group.

Staff had also noticed through their observations that Farhana was not pronouncing some of her sounds and was difficult to understand.

On reflection

The setting SENCO, the manager and parents met to discuss their concerns over the recent changes in Farhana's behaviour. Her parents reported that nothing had changed at home but they were concerned that Farhana did not want to come to the setting anymore. This was difficult as both parents usually had to rush straight off to work. They too had noticed that friends outside the family were finding it difficult to understand Farhana.

When the manager and SENCO reflected they realised that Farhana's key person was off on maternity leave, temporary staff were hard to find and Farhana's group had been covered by a variety of agency staff.

A possible solution

It was agreed that another permanent member of staff would take over the group. The new key person would visit Farhana and her family at home. She would try to build a positive relationship with Farhana and her parents which would include greeting them every day and personally taking Farhana into the setting and sharing a book with her. Within two weeks Farhana was beginning to get back to her old self and staff stopped being concerned about her behaviour.

The setting staff continued to observe Farhana's language development and together with her parents decided to make a referral for a speech and language assessment. Their area SENCO helped them with this referral.

Differentiation

> *Put simply, differentiation means teaching a child in ways and at a level which match their individual learning requirements.* (Dukes and Smith, 2006: 69)

The Early Years Foundation Stage clearly outlines the need for children to learn at their own pace through practical hands-on activities. The Practice Guidance for the EYFS gives sound advice on how practitioners can do this.

On reflection

Questions to support reflection

When practitioners have concerns about a child's progress they need to reflect upon the child's experience in their setting. They should ask themselves:

▶ What types of activities are being offered?

▶ Are they appropriate to the child's needs?

▶ Do they allow for differences in age and stage of development?

▶ Do they take account of what has been learned about the child through observation?

▶ Do activities cater for the needs and likes of all children?

▶ Do activities cater for differing **learning styles**?

A possible solution

A sound understanding and close observance of the EYFS allows practitioners to be confident that they are providing appropriate opportunities for learning for all children. Clear leadership and mentoring by managers in all aspects of the planning cycle should keep staff focused upon meeting the needs of all children.

Note

If a differentiated curriculum does not meet all a child's needs and allow them to make progress, additional support may need to be given.

Hands-on activity

Discuss the diagram 'A Reflective Practice Chart for Setting Leaders and Managers' opposite in a staff meeting or INSET.

Reflect on each of the points as they relate to your setting.

Think about possible solutions and make a plan of what you are going to do.

Further reading

Dukes, Chris and Smith, Maggie (2006) *A Practical Guide to Pre-School Inclusion*, Hands On Guides, 2nd edn. Paul Chapman Publishing.

Meggit, Carolyn (2006) *Child Development: An Illustrated Guide*, 2nd edn. Heinemann.

Miller, Linda, Cable, Carrie and Devereux, Jane (2005) *Developing Early Years practice*, Foundation Degree Texts. David Fulton Publishers.

Paige-Smith, Alice and Craft, Anna (2007) *Developing Reflective Practice in the Early Years*. Open University Press.

A Reflective Practice Chart for Setting Leaders and Managers

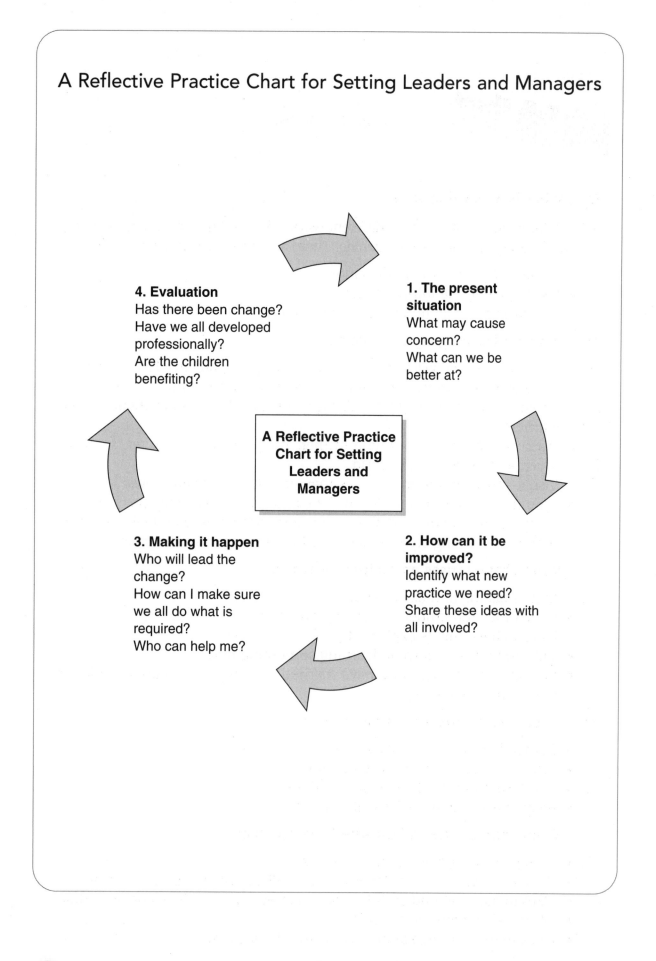

4. Evaluation
Has there been change?
Have we all developed professionally?
Are the children benefiting?

1. The present situation
What may cause concern?
What can we be better at?

A Reflective Practice Chart for Setting Leaders and Managers

3. Making it happen
Who will lead the change?
How can I make sure we all do what is required?
Who can help me?

2. How can it be improved?
Identify what new practice we need?
Share these ideas with all involved?

Recognising and Planning for Special Needs in the Early Years, SAGE © Chris Dukes and Maggie Smith, 2009

Q.   What is a learning style?

A.   Children and adults learn in different ways. Some learn best by seeing, others by hearing, and others by touching. There are three basic learning styles:

- auditory (hearing the information);
- visual (seeing the information);
- kinesthetic–tactile (touching, participation).

Q.   Why are learning styles important?

A.   • At any age, a child will learn more easily using their preferred learning style, but this doesn't mean he or she can't and won't learn any other way.
- Babies and young children all tend towards being kinesthetic–tactile learners.
- Watch a baby put everything in their mouth or a toddler reach out to touch and explore their world.
- Visual and auditory preferences may emerge as a child grows.
- Attention to learning styles will help to make learning positive and enjoyable for children. Practitioners and parents usually 'teach' in their preferred learning style, which may be different from the child's.

Q.   What characterises an auditory learner?

A.   • Enjoys talking and explanations.
- Sometimes remembers by talking out loud.
- Likes to have things explained.
- Talks to themselves while learning something new.
- Repeats new things they have learned, e.g. repeats what practitioner says during activities.

Q.   What characterises a visual learner?

A.   • Remembers visual details and enjoy stories with props or pictures.
- Prefers to see what they are learning.
- Can have trouble following instructions.
- Responds to the use of visual timetables.

Q.   What characterises a kinesthetic–tactile learner?

A.   • Prefers 'moving and doing' activities.
- Wants always to do whatever is being talked about, e.g. during a story.
- Likes to move around or 'fiddle' with something while listening or talking.
- Often 'talks' with their hands.
- Likes to touch things in order to learn about them.

CHAPTER FOUR

Development matters: looking at personal, social and emotional development

The aim of this and the following two chapters is to remind practitioners of what might be developmentally appropriate for individual children's age and stage of development.

It contains an overview of personal, social and emotional development using the developmental stages outlined in the EYFS. Each of the stages has a generous time overlap. It will enable practitioners to have appropriate expectations of the children in their care.

The chapter sets out:

▶ an overview of children's personal, social and emotional development

▶ diagrams illustrating appropriate expectations for each age range

▶ links to the relevant sections of the EYFS Practice Guidance document

▶ prompts for themed observations

and includes:

▶ points for practice

▶ a Hands-on activity

▶ further reading.

Overview

Positive personal, social and emotional development underpins all areas of a child's progress and learning. Children need to be encouraged to develop a secure sense of self as well as begin to develop the necessary skills to make friends and get along with others. Practitioners, carers and parents provide children with a secure framework which encourages respect and positive relationships; this in turn leads to children developing a strong disposition for learning.

Adults recognise that children who struggle to develop well in this area are disadvantaged and this may affect aspects of their learning. Children who find this curriculum area a challenge are invariably those who need the most support from the adults around them. In order to do this well and rise to the challenge of meeting the needs of *all* children practitioners, carers and parents need to understand fully this most important area of child development. A greater knowledge of developmental matters will allow for best practice to develop as well as provide useful insights into any difficulties a child may be experiencing.

Personal, social and emotional development and the EYFS

The **EYFS** encourages early years practitioners to implement this area of learning and development by giving attention to the following areas:

Positive Relationships

▶ Allowing children to form caring attachments

▶ Developing relationships with parents and as well as outside agencies

▶ Encouraging children and providing positive role models

▶ Planning for children in different sized groups.

Enabling Environments

▶ Ensuring a key person for all children

▶ Giving children the opportunity to develop their own interests

▶ Helping children to embrace difference

▶ Acknowledging the holistic child, including culture and religion

▶ Supporting children's independence.

Learning and Development

▶ Planning activities that promote all aspects of a child

▶ Providing experiences to encourage independence

▶ Offering a more structured approach to vulnerable children and those with behavioural or communication difficulties.

Note

*Children who have **a diagnosed or recognised condition** may be working towards a different set of criteria. In these cases practitioners should always ensure that activities are safe and suitable. This can be achieved by working in partnership with parents, therapists and any specialist teachers that may be involved with the child.*

The diagrams outlining appropriate expectations on the pages which follow offer a broad overview of the stages of personal, social and emotional development. The diagrams use as their starting points the developmental ages or stages outlined in the EYFS. Each of the stages has a generous time overlap. The stages develop as the child grows and matures and the diagrams should be read clockwise, starting at the top.

These diagrams may be used as a reference when considering your observations while the 'Prompts for Themed Observations' in the accompanying text could be used to:

▶ prompt further target observations to help clarify a concern;

▶ discuss concerns with parents;

▶ discuss concerns with other professionals such as health visitiors or other professionals. (*Note that any discussions with outside professionals should only be carried out with parental permission.*)

Remember, not all children will develop at the same pace.

Personal, Social and Emotional Development: Appropriate Expectations 0–11 Months

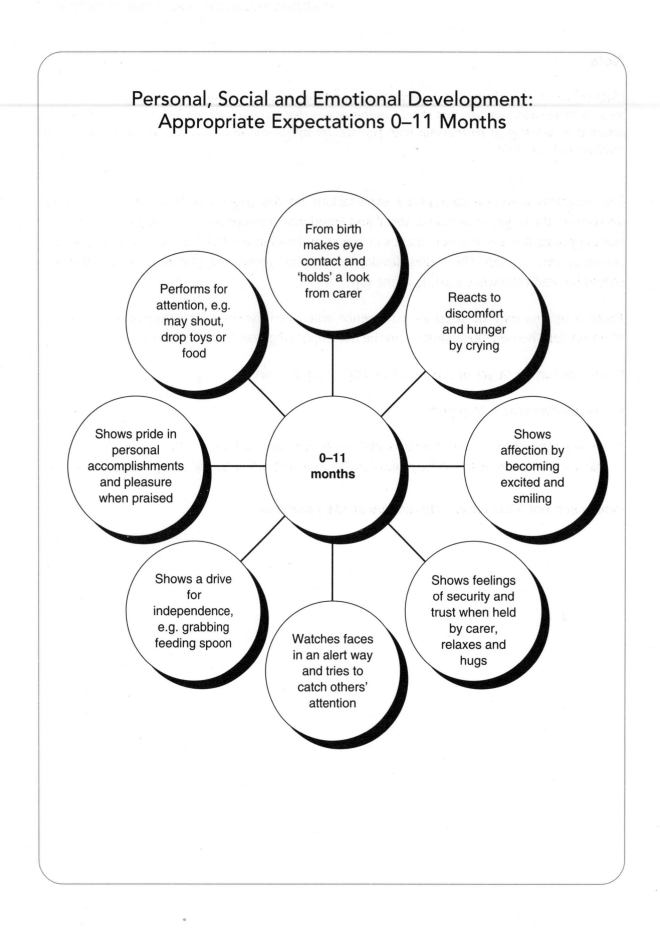

From birth makes eye contact and 'holds' a look from carer

Performs for attention, e.g. may shout, drop toys or food

Reacts to discomfort and hunger by crying

Shows pride in personal accomplishments and pleasure when praised

0–11 months

Shows affection by becoming excited and smiling

Shows a drive for independence, e.g. grabbing feeding spoon

Watches faces in an alert way and tries to catch others' attention

Shows feelings of security and trust when held by carer, relaxes and hugs

Personal, social and emotional development: 0–11 months

The Practice Guidance for the EYFS (non statutory) (pages 24–116) sets out for practitioners a series of guidelines about children's development. These are set out in useful tables. The area of Personal, Social and Emotional development can be found on pages 24–40, while pages 26, 29, 32, 35, 37 and 39 are relevant to the age range **0–11 months**.

The document reminds practitioners that:

For children, being special to someone and well cared for is vital for their physical, social and emotional health and well-being.

(EYFS Practice Guidance, page 24)

Possible prompts for themed observations

▶ A baby who does not react to hunger or discomfort.

▶ A baby who does not make any eye contact.

▶ A baby who seems continually fraught and unable to relax.

▶ A baby who doesn't seem soothed by a familiar voice when spoken to quietly and gently.

▶ A baby who doesn't make any vocalisations other than crying.

▶ A baby who doesn't vocalise to attract attention.

▶ A baby who doesn't smile at friendly familiar faces.

▶ A baby who does not laugh in response to games such as peek-a-boo or tickling games.

▶ A baby who seems lethargic and exhibits little personality.

Points for Practice

Talk with and hold babies so they can see your face and them yours. Have a two-way conversation responding to and copying any sounds they make. This positive response will build up babies' self-esteem and feelings of trust. Similarly respond quickly to babies' cries. At this age all babies need to know they can rely on and trust the adults looking after them.

Remember to praise even the youngest of babies. By doing this you are building up their self-esteem and feelings of self-worth.

Personal, Social and Emotional Development: Appropriate Expectations 8–20 Months

Smiles at faces and own reflection

Joins in a peek-a-boo game Shows anticipation and desire to explore

Can be frustrated easily, beginning tantrums but easily distracted

8–20 months

Vocalises and uses large gestures to gain attention

May be apprehensive with strangers and likes to keep carer within sight

Offers a toy or food to known adults when prompted

Feeds self with fingers Grabs spoon when being fed

Personal, social and emotional development: 8–20 months

The Practice Guidance for the EYFS (non statutory) (pages 24–116) sets out for practitioners a series of guidelines about children's development. These are set out in useful tables. The area of Personal, Social and Emotional Development can be found on pages 24–40, while pages 26, 29, 32, 35, 37 and 39 are relevant to the age range **8–20 months**.

The document reminds practitioners that:

Being acknowledged and affirmed by important people in their lives leads to children gaining confidence and inner strength through secure attachments with these people.

(EYFS Practice Guidance, page 24)

Possible prompts for themed observations

▶ A baby who does not participate in feeding by pulling, touching or trying to hold the spoon.

▶ A baby who does not progress onto lumpy food.

▶ A baby who demands little or no attention from its main caregiver.

▶ A baby who shows no possessiveness to favourite toys or people.

▶ A baby who does not show frustration and occasionally make a fuss.

▶ A baby who does not enjoy kisses and cuddles from main caregiver.

▶ A baby who is difficult to comfort.

▶ A baby who wants to do their 'own thing' all the time and does not seem to enjoy a caregiver's attention.

▶ A baby who is not developing a sense of empathy with those around, e.g. shows no concern when others are upset.

Points for Practice

This is a good age to get babies to begin to respond to simple instructions from adults. Make a game of asking the baby to give you toys and a spoonful of food. Say 'can I have some please?' and use non-verbal gesture to accompany the request, e.g. hold out your hands or open your mouth. If the baby responds positively say 'thank you very much'.

Try to set up a two-way dialogue with the baby and eventually the baby will offer you food and toys without being prompted.

This game helps develop cooperative skills and a growing sense of empathy.

Personal, Social and Emotional Development: Appropriate Expectations 16–26 Months

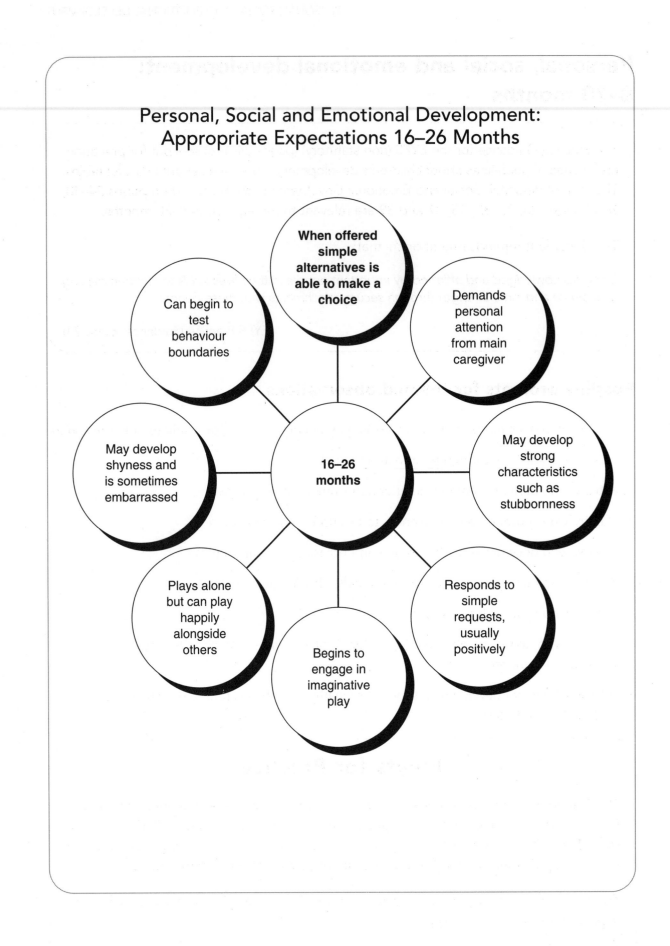

When offered simple alternatives is able to make a choice

Can begin to test behaviour boundaries

Demands personal attention from main caregiver

May develop shyness and is sometimes embarrassed

16–26 months

May develop strong characteristics such as stubbornness

Plays alone but can play happily alongside others

Begins to engage in imaginative play

Responds to simple requests, usually positively

Personal, social and emotional development: 16–26 months

The Practice Guidance for the EYFS (non statutory) (pages 24–116) sets out for practitioners a series of guidelines about children's development. These are set out in useful tables. The area of Personal, Social and Emotional Development can be found on pages 24–40, while pages 26, 29, 32–3, 35, 37 and 39 are relevant to the age range **16–26 months**.

The document reminds practitioners that:

Exploration within close relationships leads to the growth of self-assurance, promoting a sense of belonging which allows children to explore the world from a secure base.

(EYFS Practice Guidance, page 24)

Possible prompts for themed observations

▶ A toddler who shows little interest in eating and drinking.

▶ A toddler who does not participate or try 'to help' when getting dressed and undressed.

▶ A toddler who demands little attention and doesn't engage with caregivers.

▶ A toddler who is unable to amuse themselves with objects or toys for a short period.

▶ A toddler who doesn't demonstrate affection with caregiver and other familiar adults and children.

▶ A toddler who doesn't try to participate or join in during singing and nursery rhymes.

▶ A toddler who seems detached from those around.

▶ A toddler who shows little self-confidence and pride during play and activities.

▶ A toddler who shows little curiosity or desire to explore their own environment.

Points for Practice

Toddlers of this age and stage usually love to help and join in, and now is a good time to show them how to be considerate and cooperative.

Leave plenty of time for tidy-up either after a play session or meal. Support the toddler to help you put away toys or clear away dishes – they can even help with the washing up!

Try to get the toddlers to work cooperatively and support each other.

Remember to praise their efforts.

Personal, Social and Emotional Development: Appropriate Expectations 22–36 Months

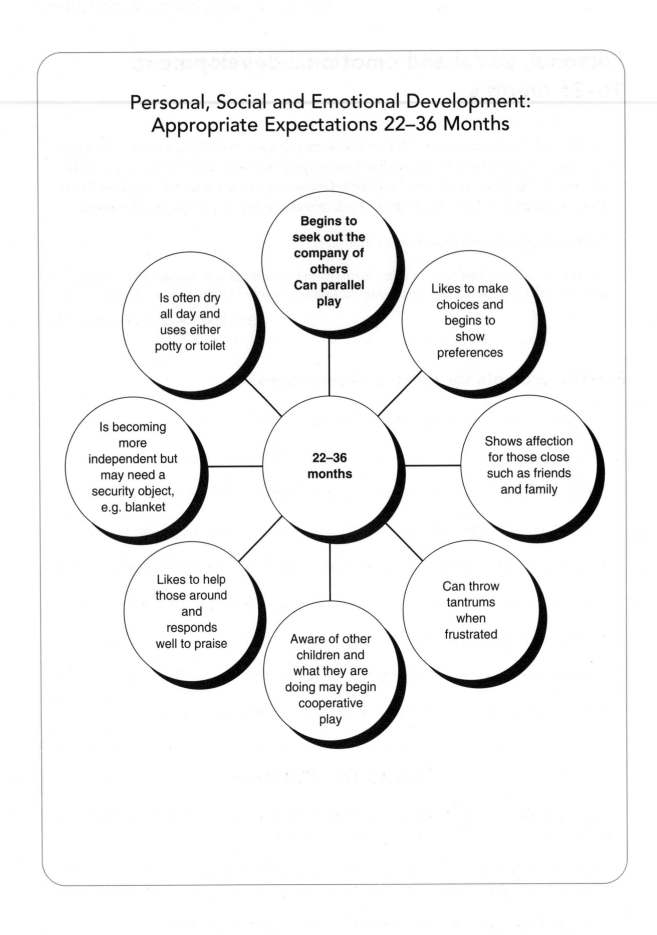

- Begins to seek out the company of others Can parallel play
- Is often dry all day and uses either potty or toilet
- Likes to make choices and begins to show preferences
- Is becoming more independent but may need a security object, e.g. blanket
- 22–36 months
- Shows affection for those close such as friends and family
- Likes to help those around and responds well to praise
- Aware of other children and what they are doing may begin cooperative play
- Can throw tantrums when frustrated

Personal, social and emotional development: 22–36 months

The Practice Guidance for the EYFS (non-statutory) (pages 24–116) sets out for practitioners a series of useful guidelines. children's development These are set out in useful tables. The area of Personal, Social and Emotional Development can be found on pages 24–40, while pages 26–7, 30, 33, 35, 37–8 and 40 are relevant to the age range **22–36 months**.

The document reminds practitioners that:

Children need adults to set a good example and to give them the opportunities for interaction with others so that they can develop positive ideas about themselves and others.

(EYFS Practice Guidance, page 24)

Possible prompts for themed observations

▶ A young child who doesn't like to join in play one on one with an adult, e.g. chasing a ball.

▶ A young child who shows no interest in feeding or dressing themselves.

▶ A young child who shows no discomfort when wearing a dirty nappy/pants.

▶ A young child who shows little interest in their peers.

▶ A young child who is non-cooperative most of the time.

▶ A young child who exhibits little self-esteem and confidence.

▶ A young child who shows little pride in any activity they have participated in, e.g. their play dough model or painting.

▶ A young child who does not seem to be aware of what is going on around them and shows little attention to dangers.

▶ A young child who shows no desire for independence and allows adults to meet their basic needs, e.g. feeding, toileting, etc.

Points for Practice

Help children of this age to join in with their friends. Join them sometimes in the imaginative play areas, perhaps to help organise a tea party. Make sure you take any shy children with you. Give the children simple chores to do in pairs to get the party set up. Encourage the children to help each other dress up and get into character for the fun ahead. Make sure you pair the shy children up with others more confident. Praise their efforts by saying things like 'I really like the way Luke and Harry are helping each other' or 'Bindi and Tanya are being so kind to each other'.

Personal, Social and Emotional Development: Appropriate Expectations 30–50 Months

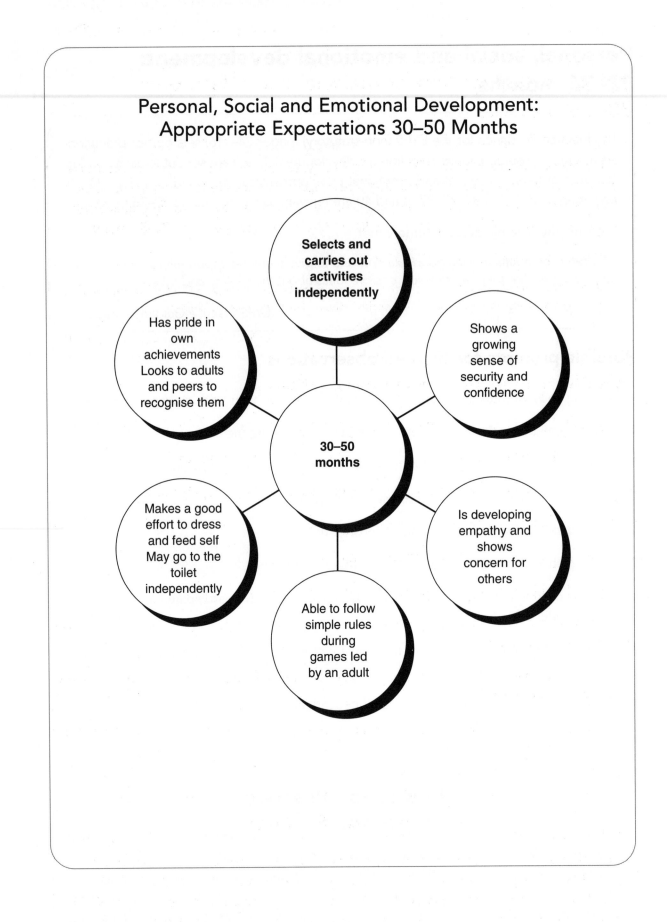

Selects and carries out activities independently

Has pride in own achievements Looks to adults and peers to recognise them

Shows a growing sense of security and confidence

30–50 months

Makes a good effort to dress and feed self May go to the toilet independently

Is developing empathy and shows concern for others

Able to follow simple rules during games led by an adult

Personal, social and emotional development: 30–50 months

The Practice Guidance for the EYFS (non statutory) (pages 24–116) sets out for practitioners a series of guidelines about children's development. These are set out in useful tables. The area of Personal, Social and Emotional Development can be found on pages 24–40, while pages 27, 30, 33, 35–6, 38 and 40 are relevant to the age range **30–50 months**.

Possible prompts for themed observations

▶ A child who finds it very difficult to cooperate with adults and peers.

▶ A child who finds separation from main carer very difficult (once given a reasonable time to settle).

▶ A child who continually throws tantrums which show no sign of lessening.

▶ A child who is not developing self-help skills, e.g. dressing, feeding, toileting.

▶ A child who cannot play and engage socially with other children for short periods.

▶ A child who is not interested in imaginative play activities.

▶ A child who wants to do the same thing all the time and who finds changes in routines difficult.

▶ A child who only plays with one or two pieces of equipment or games.

▶ A child who is difficult to motivate and who shows little interest in joining in.

Points for Practice

Create a safe and secure environment for children by establishing flexible routines and practices. Consider using a visual timetable for all the children in the setting. This will allow them to become familiar with the routines and help them anticipate what is going to happen next.

Note

Although routines are a positive thing there should always be flexibility to 'go with the flow'. Explain to children any changes that will take place, e.g. 'because of the snow (for example) we will not be going to the park this morning', or 'because you are all so busy we will have our story later', etc.

Personal Social and Emotional Development: Appropriate Expectations 40–60+ months

Developing growing concentration skills and be able to complete an activity

Shows a wide range of reactions and emotions in a confident way

Developing a sense of humour

40–60+ months

Shows care and concern for themselves, others and other living things

Able to take turns and sometimes negotiates

Chooses own friends and plays co operatively most of the time

Chooses resources and activities with intent (plan and do)

Personal, social and emotional development: 40–60+ months

The Practice Guidance for the EYFS (non-statutory) (pages 24–116) sets out for practitioners a series of guidelines about children's development. These are set out in useful tables. The area of Personal, Social and Emotional Development can be found on pages 24–40, while pages 27–8, 31, 33–4, 36, 38 and 40 are relevant to the age range **40–60+ months**.

Possible prompts for themed observations

▶ A child who prefers to work and play alone and who finds it difficult to tolerate the company of other children.

▶ A child who seems unaware of the presence of other children and ignores them.

▶ A child who is constantly bad tempered and lashes out.

▶ A child who seems withdrawn, quiet and even timid.

▶ A child who shows little initiative and waits for adults to tell them what to do next.

▶ A child who shows little interest or excitement.

▶ A child who finds it difficult to listen or give attention for even a short period of time.

▶ A child who is unaware of danger.

▶ A child who has little understanding of the consequences of their own actions or those of others.

▶ A child who is struggling with aspects of their own self-care, e.g. eating, dressing and toileting.

Points for Practice

Make the time to listen to the children's point of view at times of argument or a falling out. Giving each child their turn to tell their side of the story uninterrupted helps children feel that they are being dealt with fairly.

Note

It is not always possible for practitioners to 'solve' a problem. Sometimes it is better to help to get children to agree a compromise or best-fit solution.

Hands-on activity

The **EYFS** Practice Guidance, page 15, stresses the need more than ever for every child to have a key person to guide them.

With colleagues draw up a list of what you think the role of the key person is. Incorporate it into your information for parents.
Below are a few points to start you off (continue the bullet points):

▶ Give reassurance to children and babies
▶ Talk to parents
▶

Further reading

Dowling, Marion (2005) *Young Children's Personal, Social and Emotional Development*, 2nd edn. Paul Chapman Publishing.

Roberts, Rosemary (2006) *Self-Esteem and Early Learning: Key People from Birth to School*, Zero to Eight Series, 3rd edn. Paul Chapman Publishing.

Stocks, Sara (2002) *Personal, Social and Emotional Development (What Learning Looks Like ...)*, 2nd revised edn. Step Forward Publishing.

Visser, Jo (2007) *Supporting Personal, Social and Emotional Development*, Everything Early Years How To ... Series, Everything Early Years.

CHAPTER FIVE

Development matters: looking at communication, language and literacy

The aim of this chapter is to remind practitioners of what might be developmentally appropriate for individual children's ages and stages of development.

It contains an overview of communication, language and literacy using the developmental stages outlined in the EYFS. Each of the stages has a generous time overlap. It will enable practitioners to have appropriate expectations for the children in their care.

The chapter sets out:

▶ an overview of children's communication and language development

▶ diagrams illustrating appropriate expectations for each age range

▶ links to the relevant sections of the EYFS Practice Guidance document

▶ prompts for themed observations

and includes:

▶ points for practice

▶ a Hands-on activity

▶ further reading.

Overview

The importance of parents, carers and practitioners cannot be overestimated in identifying potential difficulties children may be experiencing in *any* areas of their development. This is especially significant in the case of communication and language development.

Research indicates that if a child who experiences difficulties in this area has their needs recognised early and interventions are forthcoming there is a strong likelihood that speedy progress and improvements can be made.

Practitioners are well placed to support any interventions by working alongside or taking note of advice from professionals such as speech and language therapists.

In order to begin to identify a child's needs parents, carers and practitioners need to be aware of the stages of child development in this most fundamental area of communication and language.

Communication, language and literacy and the EYFS

The **EYFS** encourages early years practitioners to implement this area of learning and development by giving particular attention to the following areas:

Positive Relationships

▶ Help children to communicate their thoughts, ideas and feelings

▶ Give daily opportunities to share and enjoy a wide range of fiction, songs and rhymes

▶ Role model use of language and reading and writing

▶ Identify and respond to any difficulties with language at an early stage.

Enabling Environments

▶ Plan for a language-rich environment taking into account a child's home background and culture

▶ Consider the needs of children who need alternative communications systems

▶ Provide time for conversations in a variety of ways

▶ Allow children to initiate conversations

▶ Show sensitivity and awareness of the needs of children learning English as an additional language.

Learning and Development

▶ Link language with rhymes, songs and practical experiences

▶ Show a willingness to recognise many different ways of children communicating

▶ Develop phonological awareness

▶ Develop children's awareness of other languages and communication systems such as Braille.

The diagrams outlining appropriate expectations on the pages which follow offer a broad overview of the stages of communication, language and literacy. The diagrams use as their starting points the developemental ages or stages outlined in the EYFS. Each of the stages has a generous time overlap. The stages develop as the child grows and matures and the diagrams should be read clockwise, starting at the top.

These diagrams may be used as a reference when considering your observations while the 'Prompts for Themed Observations' in the accompanying text could be used to:

▶ prompt further target observations to help clarify a concern;

▶ discuss concerns with parents;

▶ discuss concerns with other professionals. (*Note that any discussions with outside professionals should only be carried out with parental permission*).

Remember, not all children will develop at the same pace.

Note

*Children who have **a diagnosed or recognised condition** may be working towards a different set of criteria. In these cases practitioners should always ensure that activities and expectations are suitable. This can be achieved by working in partnership with parents, therapists and any specialist teachers that may be involved with the child.*

Communication, Language and Literacy Development: Appropriate Expectations 0–11 Months

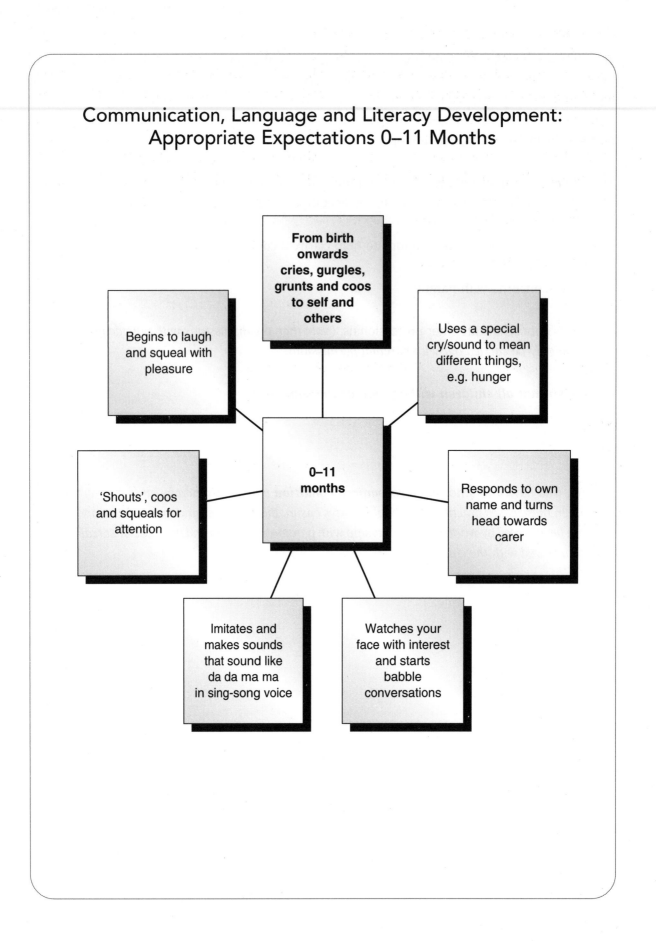

From birth onwards cries, gurgles, grunts and coos to self and others

Begins to laugh and squeal with pleasure

Uses a special cry/sound to mean different things, e.g. hunger

0–11 months

'Shouts', coos and squeals for attention

Responds to own name and turns head towards carer

Imitates and makes sounds that sound like da da ma ma in sing-song voice

Watches your face with interest and starts babble conversations

Communication, language and literacy: 0–11 months

The Practice Guidance for the EYFS (non-statutory) (pages 24–116) sets out for practitioners a series of guidelines about children's development. These are set out in useful tables. The area of Communication, Language and Literacy can be found on pages 41–62, while pages 43, 49, 52, 55, 59, and 61 are relevant to the age range **0–11 months**.

The document reminds practitioners that:

Parents and immediate family members most easily understand their babies' and children's communications and can often interpret for others.

(EYFS Practice Guidance, page 39)

Possible prompts for themed observations

▶ A baby who does not smile.

▶ A baby who does not cry to express hunger or pain.

▶ A baby who does not turn their head towards a voice or sound.

▶ A baby who does not vocalise or babble.

▶ A baby who does not follow a moving object with their eyes.

▶ A baby who does not interact with their carer during games such as peek-a-boo.

▶ A baby who has no reaction to sudden noises.

Points for Practice

Mimic any sounds a baby makes back to them. This encourages a baby to communicate more. Make eye contact, smile and have a conversation. This shows you are acknowledging and appreciating their efforts.

Remember to tell parents about the various ways their child has been communicating during the day while with you. This flow of conversation helps build trusting relationships between practitioners and carers. It shows parents that you give time and attention to their child and recognise their individual qualities.

Communication, Language and Literacy Development: Appropriate Expectations 8–20 Months

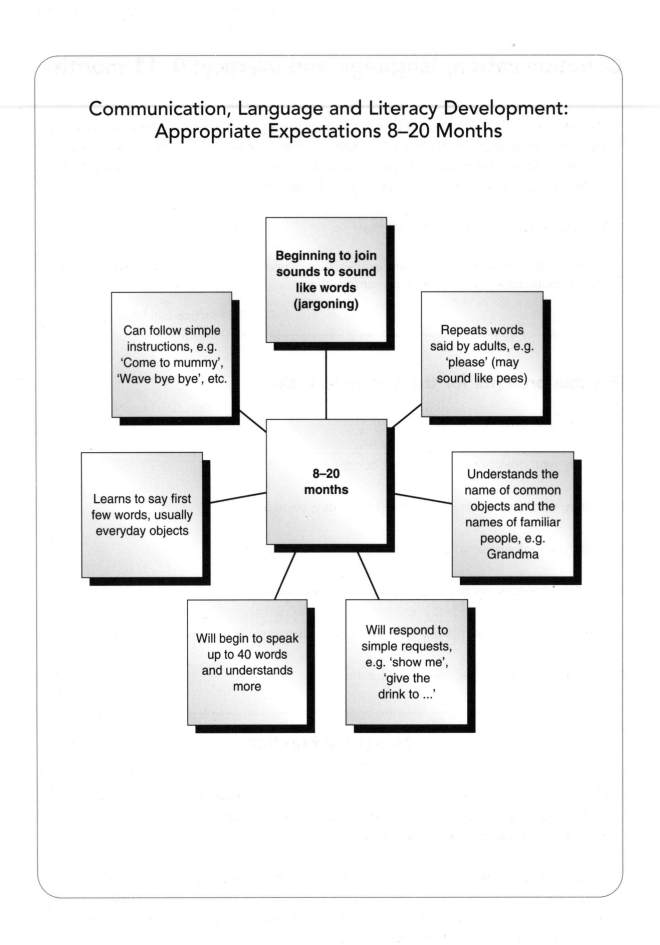

Beginning to join sounds to sound like words (jargoning)

Can follow simple instructions, e.g. 'Come to mummy', 'Wave bye bye', etc.

Repeats words said by adults, e.g. 'please' (may sound like pees)

Learns to say first few words, usually everyday objects

8–20 months

Understands the name of common objects and the names of familiar people, e.g. Grandma

Will begin to speak up to 40 words and understands more

Will respond to simple requests, e.g. 'show me', 'give the drink to ...'

Communication, language and literacy: 8–20 months

The Practice Guidance for the EYFS (non-statutory) (pages 24–116) sets out for practitioners a series of guidelines about children's development. These are set out in useful tables. The area of Communication, Language and Literacy can be found on pages 41–62, while pages 43, 49, 52, 55, 59 and 61 are relevant to the age range **8–20 months**.

The document reminds practitioners that:

To become skilful communicators, babies and children need to be with people who have meaning for them and with whom they have warm and loving relationships, such as their family or carers and, in a group situation, a key person whom they know and trust.

(EYFS Practice Guidance, page 41)

Possible prompts for themed observations

▶ A baby who does not produce lots of sounds or babbles.

▶ A baby who does not respond or turn their head towards a voice.

▶ A baby who does not have much interest in what is going on around them.

▶ A baby who shows little in interest in communicating or playing with a caring adult.

▶ A baby who seems to demand little attention and who does not use their voice to get the adults' attention.

▶ A baby who shows little excitement.

▶ A baby who has no single words (in any language) by 16 months.

▶ A baby who suddenly stops using words.

Points for Practice

General reference words should be role-modelled by practitioners, parents and carers.

These are the first words used to reflect routines and objects that a child is already familiar with. By hearing the same words over again the child will begin to anticipate and eventually use the words themselves.

They could include 'juice' (meaning all drinks), 'story', 'home time' (meaning time to go home or that a parent is about to arrive), 'changing time' (meaning time for some type of personal care routine), etc. It is often useful if all practitioners use the same broad phrases within a setting.

Communication, Language and Literacy Development: Appropriate Expectations 16–26 Months

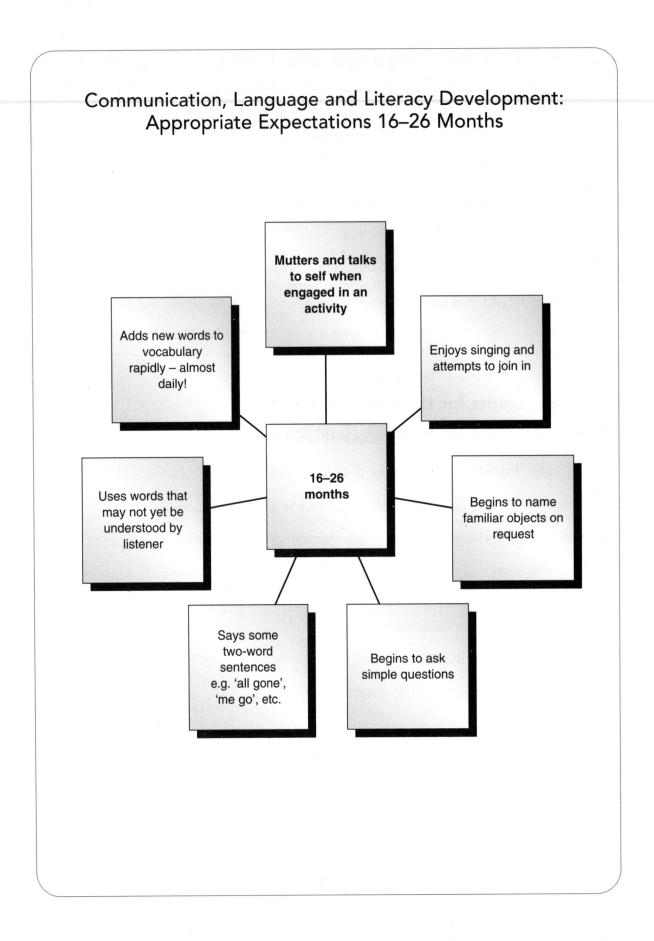

Mutters and talks to self when engaged in an activity

Adds new words to vocabulary rapidly – almost daily!

Enjoys singing and attempts to join in

16–26 months

Uses words that may not yet be understood by listener

Begins to name familiar objects on request

Says some two-word sentences e.g. 'all gone', 'me go', etc.

Begins to ask simple questions

Communication, language and literacy: 16–26 months

The Practice Guidance for the EYFS (non-statutory) sets out for practitioners a series of guidelines about children's development. These are set out in useful tables. The area of Communication, Language and Literacy can be found on pages 41–62, while pages 44, 49, 52, 55, 59 and 61 are relevant to the age range **16–26 months**.

The document reminds practitioners that:

Babies and children use their voices to make contact and to let people know what they need and how they feel, establishing their own identities and personalities.

(EYFS Practice Guidance, page 41)

Possible prompts for themed observations

▶ A child who uses more gestures than words to communicate.

▶ A child who does not try to get attention from a caring adult, e.g. does not pull the adult to look.

▶ A child who does not seem to understand words for everyday familiar objects.

▶ A child who is very quiet.

▶ A child who is not putting or beginning to put two words together.

▶ A child who cannot listen and respond to simple instructions.

▶ A child who does not volunteer basic information.

▶ A child who does not have 20 plus words that they use regularly (in any language).

Points for Practice

Children of this age have usually started to be able to name single objects so this is a good time for parents, practitioners and carers to introduce the *function of an object*. For example, when a child says 'hat' extend the conversation by saying 'your *hat* for keeping your head warm'. Similarly, if a child says 'juice', extend by saying '*juice* for you to drink'. This will support young children to develop their own descriptive language.

Communication, Language and Literacy Development:
Appropriate Expectations 22–36 Months

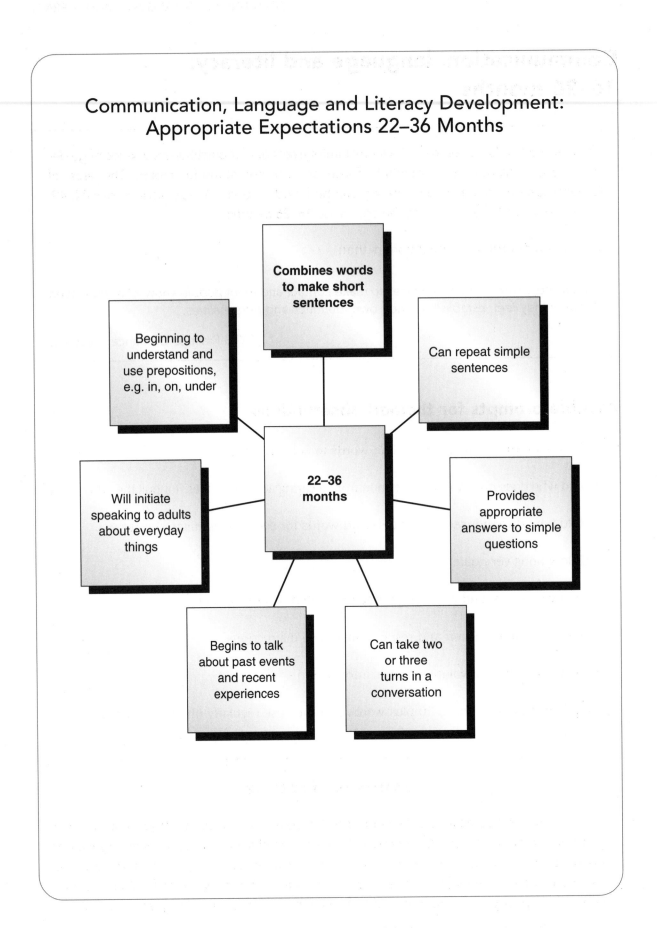

Combines words to make short sentences

Beginning to understand and use prepositions, e.g. in, on, under

Can repeat simple sentences

22–36 months

Will initiate speaking to adults about everyday things

Provides appropriate answers to simple questions

Begins to talk about past events and recent experiences

Can take two or three turns in a conversation

Communication, language and literacy: 22–36 months

The **Practice Guidance for the EYFS** (non-statutory) (pages 24–116) sets out for practitioners a series of guidelines about children's development. These are set out in useful tables. The area of Communication, Language and Literacy can be found on pages 41–62, while pages 44–5, 49, 52–3, 55, 59 and 61 are relevant to the age range **22–36 months**.

The document reminds practitioners that:

All children learn best through activities and experiences that engage all the senses. For example, music, dance, rhythms and son's play a key role in language development.

(EYFS Practice Guidance, page 41)

Possible prompts for themed observations

▶ A child who has difficulty following simple instructions.

▶ A child who relies heavily on following others or using non-verbal clues to follow instructions (if instructions are in the child's first language).

▶ A child who is withdrawn or quiet on a consistent basis.

▶ A child who only uses one- or two-word phrases.

▶ A child who shows frustration when trying to talk.

▶ A child who is difficult for familiar adults to understand.

▶ A child who is stammering (i.e. has periods of stammering over a few weeks long).

▶ A child with poor listening skills (who cannot 'listen' for more than a couple of minutes).

Points for Practice

To help children develop good listening skills keep group sizes small and offer opportunities for one-on-one stories and play. Remember that children this young cannot be expected to sit listening for too long so try to make all sessions interactive by using pop-up books, story sacks and puppets.

When introducing children to new songs and nursery rhymes try to include those that have repeated lines and verses. Young children find these easier to learn and have more fun joining in.

Remember to inform parents which songs and rhymes you are teaching so they can reinforce and enjoy their learning at home.

Communication, Language and Literacy Development: Appropriate Expectations 30–50 Months

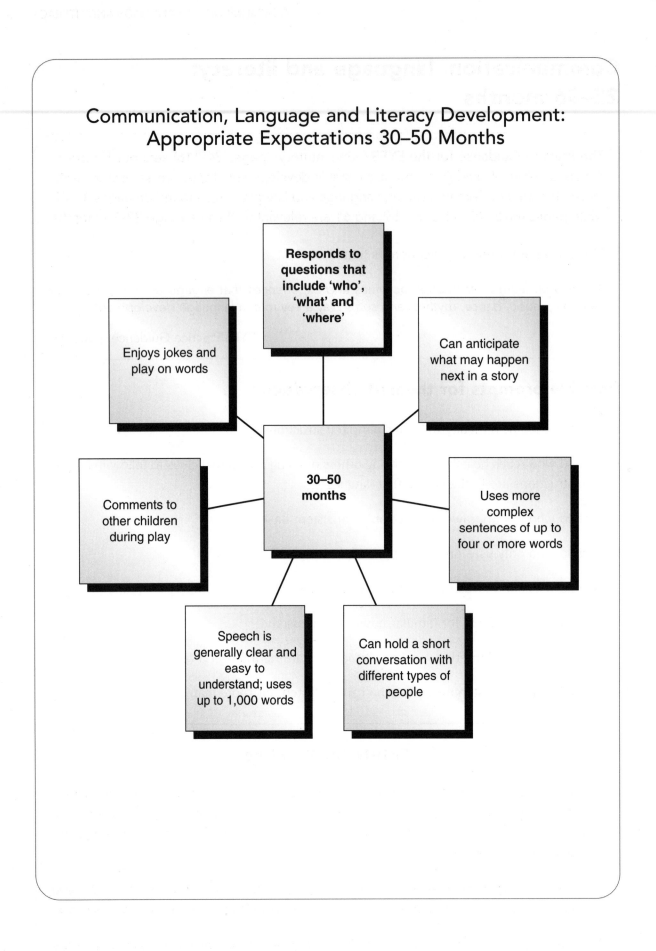

Responds to questions that include 'who', 'what' and 'where'

Enjoys jokes and play on words

Can anticipate what may happen next in a story

Comments to other children during play

30–50 months

Uses more complex sentences of up to four or more words

Speech is generally clear and easy to understand; uses up to 1,000 words

Can hold a short conversation with different types of people

Communication, language and literacy: 30–50 months

The Practice Guidance for the EYFS (non-statutory) (pages 24–116) sets out for practitioners a series of guidelines about children's development. These are set out in useful tables. The area of Communication, Language and Literacy can be found on pages 41–62, while pages 45–6, 50, 53, 56, 59–60 and 61 are relevant to the age range **30–50 months.**

The document reminds practitioners that:

Communicating and being with others helps children to build social relationships which provide opportunities for friendship, empathy and sharing emotions. The ability to communicate helps children to participate more fully in society.

(EYFS Practice Guidance, page 41)

Possible prompts for themed observations

▶ A child who is unable to follow simple clear instructions.

▶ A child who seems not to be able to comprehend what others are saying.

▶ A child unable to concentrate and listen for more than a few minutes.

▶ A child with a small vocabulary who finds it hard to construct a sentence.

▶ A child who is unable to understand a simple question such as 'what's this?'

▶ A child whose speech is difficult to understand even by familiar adults.

▶ A child who is stammering (i.e. has periods of stammering over a few weeks long).

Points for Practice

To help children develop good listening skills keep group sizes small and offer opportunities for one-on-one stories and play. Remember that children this young cannot be expected to sit listening for too long so try to make all sessions interactive by using pop-up books, story sacks and puppets.

When introducing children to new songs and nursery rhymes try to include those that have repeated lines and verses. Young children find these easier to learn and have more fun joining in.

Remember to inform parents which songs and rhymes you are teaching so they can reinforce and enjoy their learning at home.

Communication, Language and Literacy Development: Appropriate Expectations 40–60+ Months

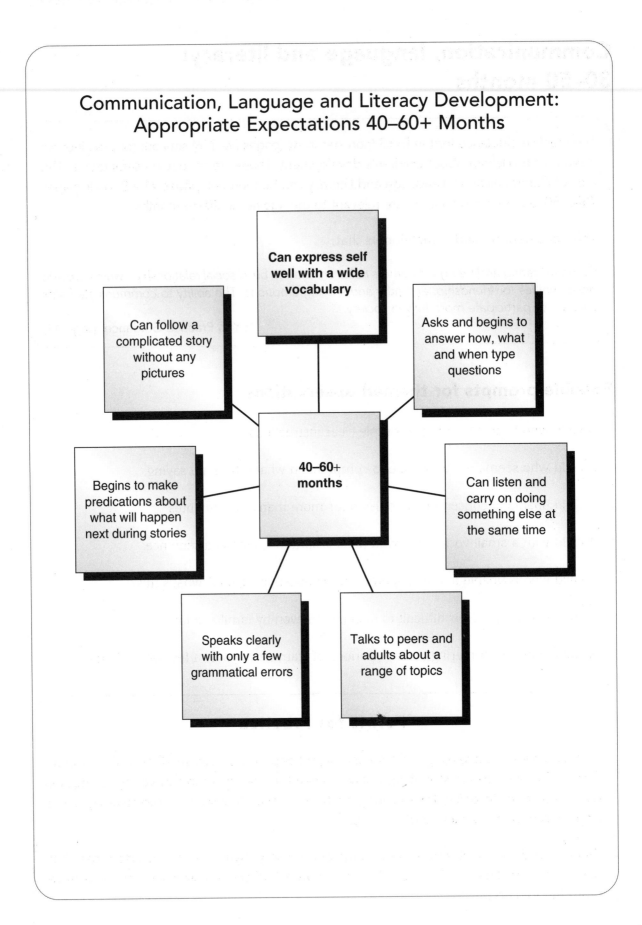

Can express self well with a wide vocabulary

Can follow a complicated story without any pictures

Asks and begins to answer how, what and when type questions

40–60+ months

Begins to make predications about what will happen next during stories

Can listen and carry on doing something else at the same time

Speaks clearly with only a few grammatical errors

Talks to peers and adults about a range of topics

Communication, language and literacy: 40–60+ months

The Practice Guidance for the EYFS (non-statutory) sets out for practitioners a series of guidelines about children's development. These are set out in useful tables. The area of Communication, Language and Literacy can be found on pages 41–62, while pages 47–8, 50–1, 53–4, 57–8, 60 and 62 are relevant to the age range **40–60+ months**.

The document reminds practitioners that:

As children develop speaking and listening skills they build the foundations for literacy, for making sense of visual and verbal signs and ultimately for reading and writing. Children need lots of opportunities to interact with others as they develop these skills, and to use a wide variety of resources for expressing their understanding, including mark making, drawing, modelling, reading and writing.

(EYFS Practice Guidance, page 41)

Possible prompts for themed observations

▶ A child who does not seem to understand simple instructions.

▶ A child who is unable to hold a simple conversation in their own first language.

▶ A child who does not use complete simple sentences.

▶ A child with poor listening and attention skills.

▶ A child who cannot follow or retell a simple familiar story.

▶ A child who doesn't ask questions.

▶ A child who does not use language to interact with peers during play.

▶ A child whose speech is unclear to others.

▶ A child with a limited vocabulary.

▶ A child who does not listen or contribute to relevant discussions (with known peers and adults).

▶ A child who stammers (i.e. has periods of stammering lasting more than a few weeks).

Points for Practice

Plan for activities that develop children's *listening and attention* skills daily such as board games, 'Simon says' type movement games, story tapes, nature walks, small-circle time and show and tell.

Hands-on activity

Observing language skills

Make time to carry out targeted observations on every child's communication and language skills. These observations can be done in a variety of ways, e.g.

▶ a targeted observation over a 20-minute period noting down the language (verbal and non-verbal) a child is using;

▶ by using a tracking format in which it is noted when, how and who a child communicates with over a specific period;

▶ by encouraging children to re-tell a favourite story, using a picture book or story sack, into a tape recorder – listen closely afterwards for clarity of speech and use of vocabulary.

Further reading

Dukes, Chris and Smith, Maggie (2007) *Developing Pre-school Communication and Language*, Hands On Guides, 2nd edn. Paul Chapman Publishing.

Meggitt, Carolyn (2006) *Child Development: An Illustrated Guide*, 2nd edn. Heinemann.

Sharp, Elizabeth (2005) *Learning Through Talk in the Early Years: Practical Activities for the Classroom*. Paul Chapman Publishing.

CHAPTER SIX

Development matters: looking at physical development

The aim of this chapter is to remind practitioners of what might be developmentally appropriate for individual children's ages and stages of development.

It contains an overview of physical development using the developmental stages outlined in the EYFS. Each of the stages has a generous time overlap. It will enable practitioners to have appropriate expectations for the children in their care.

The chapter sets out:

▶ an overview of children's physical development

▶ diagrams illustrating appropriate expectations for each age range

▶ links to the relevant sections of the EYFS Practice Guidance document

▶ prompts for themed observations

and includes:

▶ points for practice

▶ a Hands-on activity

▶ further reading.

Overview

Babies are born with some instinctive reflexes such as sucking. However after birth all other physical movements are learned. As parents, carers and practitioners our role is to provide babies and youngsters with the opportunities to improve their physical skills as well as develop healthy choices in relation to food, rest and exercise.

Children who experience difficulties with any aspects of physical development can be enormously supported in the early years. The focus on outdoor and large-apparatus play as well as the countless activities that help develop fine motor skills provide the cornerstones of early years practice. In order to provide babies and youngsters with suitable opportunities for physical advancement practitioners, carers and parents, need to have a firm grasp of the patterns of physical development.

This knowledge about developmental matters will enable best practice to follow as well as begin to highlight any difficulties a child may be encountering.

Physical development and the EYFS

The **EYFS** encourages early years practitioners to implement this area of learning and development by giving attention to the following:

Positive Relationships

▶ Build children's confidence

▶ Motivate children to be active

▶ Notice and value those things children do spontaneously

▶ Provide children with an understanding of health and hygiene matters.

Enabling Environments

▶ Provide interesting and challenging resources

▶ Allow for energetic play

▶ Work in partnership with physiotherapists and any other therapists a child may have

▶ Give additional support to those children who need it.

Learning and Development

▶ Plan challenging activities

▶ Give children time to practise and learn new skills

▶ Introduce any relevant language to accompany new physical skills

▶ Help children make healthy food choices.

Note

Children who have a diagnosed or recognised physical condition may be working towards a different set of criteria. In these cases practitioners should always ensure that activities are safe and suitable. This can be achieved by working in partnership with parents, therapists and any specialist teachers that may be involved with the child.

The diagrams outlining appropriate expectations on the pages which follow offter a broad overview of the stages of physical development. The diagrams use as their starting points the developmental ages or stages outlined in the EYFS. Each of the stages has a generous time overlap. The stages develop as the child grows and matures and the diagrams should be read clockwise, starting at the top.

These diagrams may be used as a reference when considering your observations while the 'Prompts for Themed Observations' in the accompanying text could be used to:

▶ prompt further target observations to help clarify a concern;

▶ discuss concerns with parents;

▶ discuss concerns with other professionals such as health visitiors or other professionals. (*Note that any discussions with outside professionals should only be carried out with parental permission.*)

Remember, not all children will develop at the same pace.

Physical Development:
Appropriate Expectations 0–11 Months

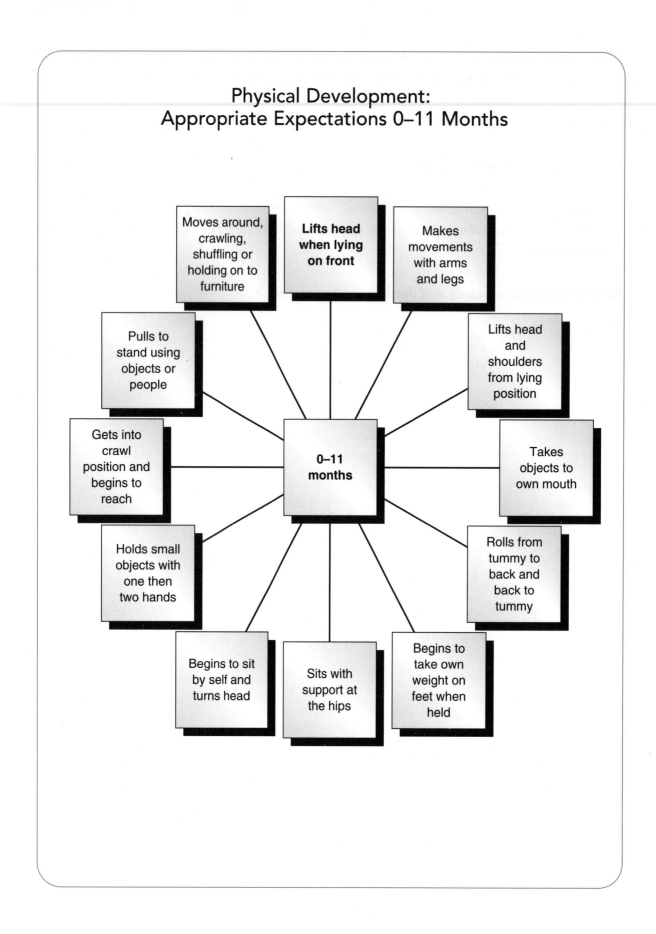

Moves around, crawling, shuffling or holding on to furniture

Lifts head when lying on front

Makes movements with arms and legs

Lifts head and shoulders from lying position

Pulls to stand using objects or people

Gets into crawl position and begins to reach

0–11 months

Takes objects to own mouth

Holds small objects with one then two hands

Rolls from tummy to back and back to tummy

Begins to sit by self and turns head

Sits with support at the hips

Begins to take own weight on feet when held

Physical development: 0–11 months

The Practice Guidance for the EYFS (non-statutory) (pages 24–116) sets out for practitioners a series of guidelines about children's development. These are set out in useful tables. The area of Physical Development can be found on pages 92–105, while pages 94, 99 and 103 are relevant to the age range **0–11 months**.

The document reminds practitioners that:

Babies and children learn from being active and Physical Development takes place across all areas of Learning and Development.

(EYFS Practice Guidance, page 92)

Possible prompts for themed observations

▶ A baby who does not play with their fingers, hands and toes.

▶ A baby with poor unexplained sucking and little mouthing (i.e. putting objects into mouth).

▶ A baby who does not hold up their head for a short time and who does not try to raise him/herself up on forearms.

▶ A baby who makes little attempt to roll from back to side and onto tummy.

▶ A baby who does not reach out to touch or grab people or objects.

▶ A baby who cannot sit without a lot of support.

▶ A baby who does not begin to develop hand–eye coordination.

Points for practice

When changing a baby's nappy, if there is time, leave the nappy off for a few minutes and let the baby enjoy kicking and stretching.

Encourage a baby to stretch out for those things they may want. When the baby is lying on the floor put favourite toys just out of reach and show the baby how to stretch their arms to reach them.

Introduce simple action songs to the baby. Show the baby how to make the finger and hand movements and praise their efforts. Sing songs like 'The Wheels on the Bus' or simply clap along to story tapes.

Physical Development:
Appropriate Expectations 8–20 Months

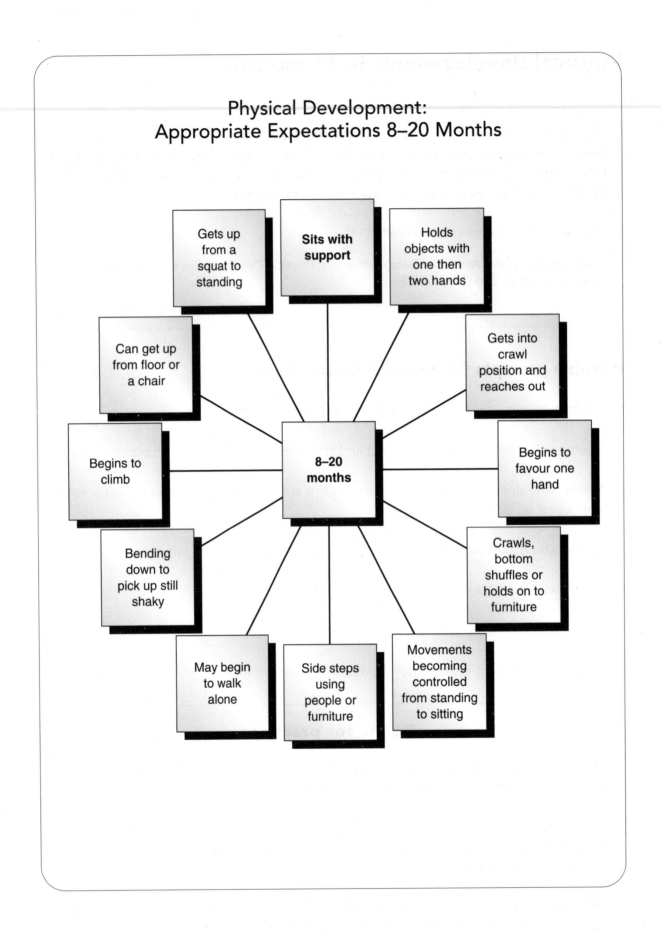

Gets up from a squat to standing

Sits with support

Holds objects with one then two hands

Can get up from floor or a chair

Gets into crawl position and reaches out

Begins to climb

8–20 months

Begins to favour one hand

Bending down to pick up still shaky

Crawls, bottom shuffles or holds on to furniture

May begin to walk alone

Side steps using people or furniture

Movements becoming controlled from standing to sitting

Physical development: 8–20 months

The Practice Guidance for the EYFS (non-statutory) sets out for practitioners a series of guidelines about children's development. These are set out in useful tables. The area of Physical Development can be found on pages 92–105, while pages 94, 99 and 103 are relevant to the age range **8–20 months**.

The document reminds practitioners that:

Good health care in the early years helps to safeguard health and well-being throughout life. It is important that children develop healthy habits when they first learn about food and activity. Growing with appropriate weight gain in the first years of life helps to guard against obesity in later life.

(EYFS Practice Guidance, page 92)

Possible prompts for themed observations

▶ A baby/toddler who does not try to move around either by crawling, bottom shuffling or walking.

▶ A baby/toddler who does not use a palmer (whole hand) then a pincer grasp (finger and thumb).

▶ A baby/toddler who does not transfer objects from hand to hand.

▶ A baby/toddler who does not develop fine motor skills such as beginning to build with bricks, hold chunky books, etc.

▶ A baby/toddler who makes no attempt to feed themselves when encouraged with finger foods.

▶ A baby/toddler who does not stretch, begin to climb or display large motor physical activity.

Points for practice

Once a baby/toddler starts pulling to their feet and developing balance put secure objects such as furniture in a line to allow them to begin to move around safely while holding on. Not only is it a fun game but it strengthens muscles and improves balance.

Note

Always be available to support or 'catch' a baby who is beginning to toddle.

Physical Development:
Appropriate Expectations 16–26 Months

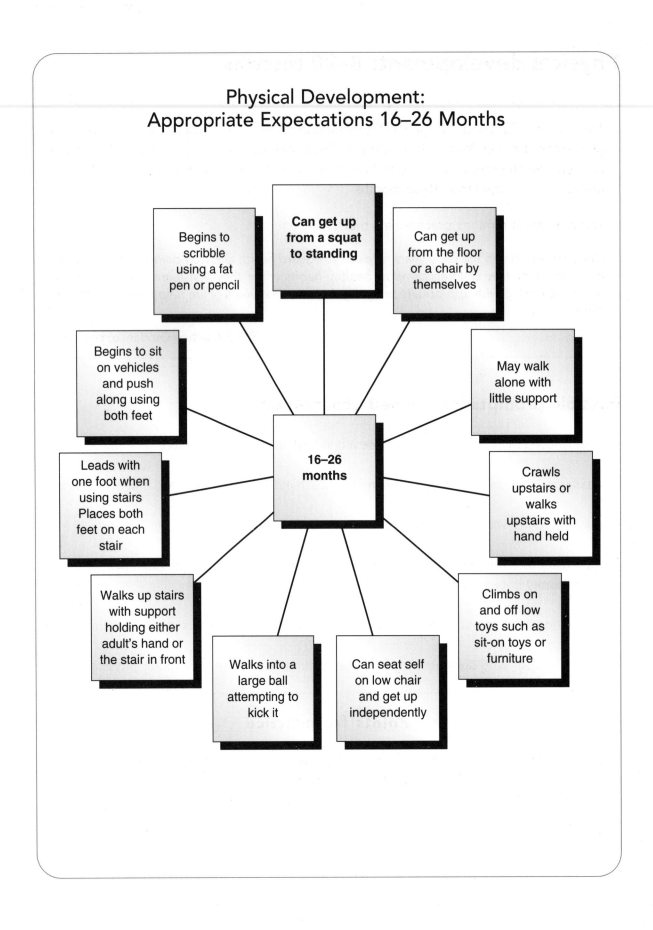

Begins to scribble using a fat pen or pencil

Can get up from a squat to standing

Can get up from the floor or a chair by themselves

Begins to sit on vehicles and push along using both feet

May walk alone with little support

16–26 months

Leads with one foot when using stairs Places both feet on each stair

Crawls upstairs or walks upstairs with hand held

Walks up stairs with support holding either adult's hand or the stair in front

Climbs on and off low toys such as sit-on toys or furniture

Walks into a large ball attempting to kick it

Can seat self on low chair and get up independently

Physical development: 16–26 months

The Practice Guidance for the EYFS (non-statutory) (pages 24–114) sets out for practitioners a series of guidelines about children's development. These are set out in useful tables. The area of Physical Development can be found on pages 92–105, while pages 94–5, 100 and 103 are relevant to the age range **16–26 months**.

Possible prompts for themed observations

▶ A toddler who has poor balance and falls over a lot from a standing position.

▶ A toddler who needs to be picked up or pulled onto feet.

▶ A toddler not using both hands, e.g. steadies toy with one hand when using the other to explore an object.

▶ A toddler who does not get up and begin to try to move around.

▶ A toddler who does not begin to climb.

▶ A toddler who does not find a way to get up and down stairs.

▶ A toddler who continues to walk with a stiff gait.

Points for practice

Practitioners often anticipate the needs of the children in their care. Try to make sure you sometimes leave objects a child wants out of their reach and encourage them to stand up and walk towards the object. Remember to praise them for their efforts.

Encourage outdoor play for toddlers but remember to have climbing activities, pull and push type toys as well as sit on and ride toys indoors.

Physical Development:
Appropriate Expectations 22–36 Months

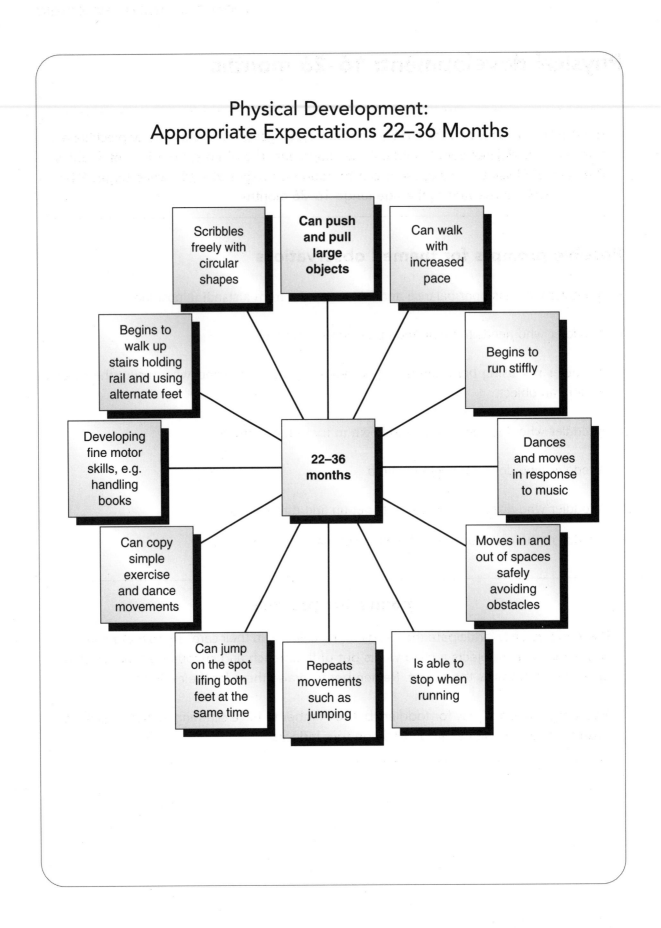

Scribbles freely with circular shapes

Can push and pull large objects

Can walk with increased pace

Begins to walk up stairs holding rail and using alternate feet

Begins to run stiffly

Developing fine motor skills, e.g. handling books

22–36 months

Dances and moves in response to music

Can copy simple exercise and dance movements

Moves in and out of spaces safely avoiding obstacles

Can jump on the spot lifing both feet at the same time

Repeats movements such as jumping

Is able to stop when running

Physical development: 22–36 months

The Practice Guidance for the EYFS (non-statutory) sets out for practitioners a series of guidelines about children's development. These are set out in useful tables. The area of Physical Development can be found on pages 92–105, while pages 95–6, 100 and 103–4 are relevant to the age range **22–36 months**.

The document reminds practitioners that:

Physical development helps children to develop a positive sense of well-being.

(EYFS Practice Guidance, page 92)

Possible prompts for themed observations

▶ A young child who constantly bumps into objects both indoors and outdoors.

▶ A young child who is always dropping things and who has poor fine motor control.

▶ A young child who can't stop safely when running.

▶ A young child who is lacking in confidence when undertaking physical activity.

▶ A young child who has trouble getting up and down the stairs.

▶ A young child who cannot complete simple inset puzzles (2–5 pieces) with support.

▶ A young child who has difficulty joining in simple action songs.

▶ A young child who cannot throw objects.

Points for Practice

Practise simple action songs such as 'Incy Wincey Spider' and 'The Wheels on the Bus' every day.

Introduce simple dance and exercise sessions when children copy your movements. Make the movements big and easy to do.

Offer a 'helping hand' during physical exercise such as walking along a balancing beam but try to reduce the support to a 'helping finger' until eventually the child moves independently.

Physical Development:
Appropriate Expectations 30–50 Months

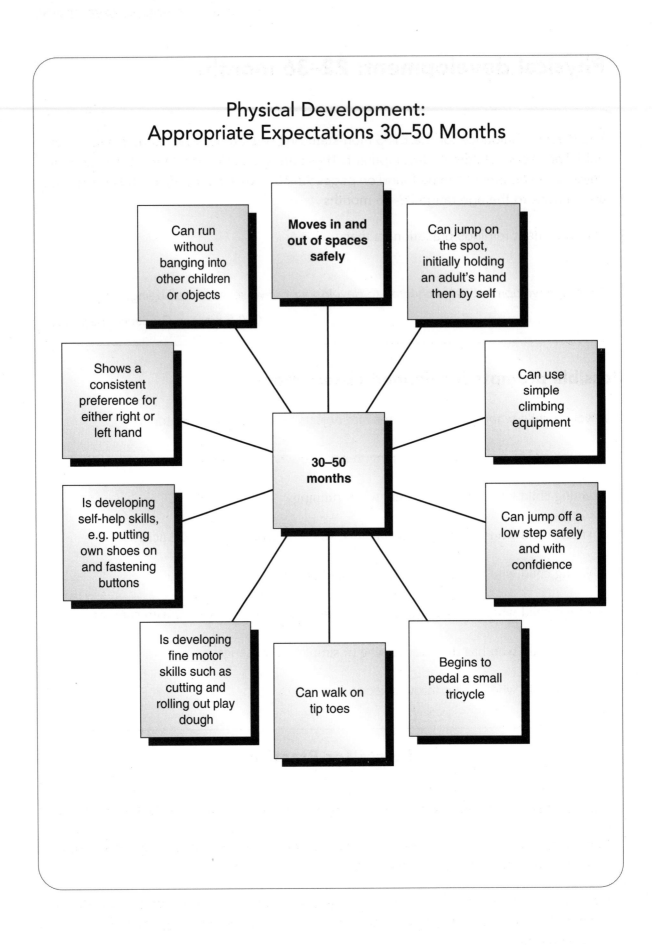

Can run without banging into other children or objects

Moves in and out of spaces safely

Can jump on the spot, initially holding an adult's hand then by self

Shows a consistent preference for either right or left hand

Can use simple climbing equipment

Is developing self-help skills, e.g. putting own shoes on and fastening buttons

30–50 months

Can jump off a low step safely and with confdience

Is developing fine motor skills such as cutting and rolling out play dough

Can walk on tip toes

Begins to pedal a small tricycle

Physical development: 30–50 months

The Practice Guidance for the EYFS (non-statutory) sets out for practitioners a series of guidelines about children's development. These are set out in useful tables. The area of Physical Development can be found on pages 92–105, while pages 96–7, 101 and 104 are relevant to the age range **30–50 months**.

The document reminds practitioners that:

Physical Development helps children gain confidence in what they can do.

(EYFS Practice Guidance, page 92)

Possible prompts for themed observations

▶ A child who is still bumping into people and objects when walking or running.

▶ A child who appears clumsy, e.g. who drops things, fumbles and trips.

▶ A child with poor balance, e.g. cannot balance on one foot for a short time.

▶ A child who cannot throw a ball.

▶ A child who cannot draw scribbles, simple circles or hold a fat pen or pencil.

▶ A child with poor self-help skills, e.g. does not attempt to dress themselves.

▶ A child who cannot copy simple actions and movements.

Points for Practice

Try to make sure that younger children get access to wheeled vehicles such as tricycles and scooters by giving them their own play sessions in a quiet outside area where they can practise their skills.

Introduce a system which will allows for fair sharing of equipment. Consider using a large sand timer for the most desirable equipment so that everyone will get a turn.

This is the age/stage when children will be rapidly developing their fine motor abilities. Make sure to have plenty of activities on offer that allow them to practise their skills. A creative workshop with a variety of materials provides many opportunities for children in this area of development.

Physical Development:
Appropriate Expectations 40–60+ Months

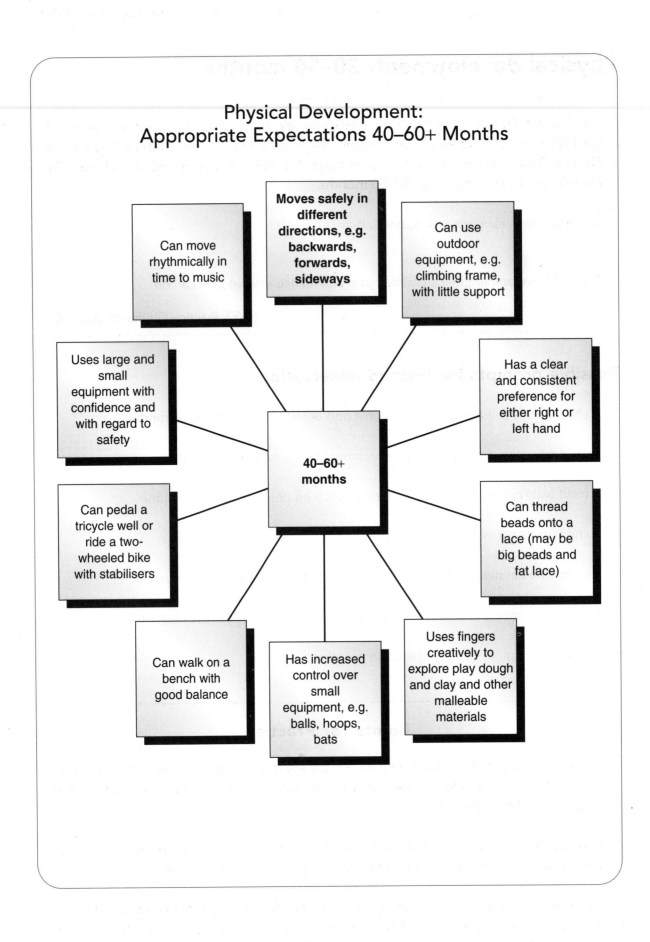

Moves safely in different directions, e.g. backwards, forwards, sideways

Can move rhythmically in time to music

Can use outdoor equipment, e.g. climbing frame, with little support

Uses large and small equipment with confidence and with regard to safety

Has a clear and consistent preference for either right or left hand

40–60+ months

Can pedal a tricycle well or ride a two-wheeled bike with stabilisers

Can thread beads onto a lace (may be big beads and fat lace)

Can walk on a bench with good balance

Has increased control over small equipment, e.g. balls, hoops, bats

Uses fingers creatively to explore play dough and clay and other malleable materials

Physical development: 40–60+ months

The Practice Guidance for the EYFS (non-statutory) (pages 24–116) sets out for practitioners a series of guidelines about children's development. These are set out in useful tables. The area of Physical Development can be found on pages 92–105, while pages 97–8, 101–2 and 105 are relevant to the age range **40–60+ months**.

The document reminds practitioners that they should:

Build children's confidence to take manageable risks in their play.

(EYFS Practice Guidance, page 92)

Possible prompts for themed observations

▶ A child who has difficulty with balance and falls over frequently.

▶ A child who finds handling small equipment difficult, e.g. scissors, jigsaws, fat pens and pencils, turning the pages of a book, etc.

▶ A child who has poor self-help skills, e.g. putting shoes and coat on.

▶ A child who can move fast but has little control when stopping.

▶ A child who appears fearless and pays little attention to physical dangers or the safety of themselves or others.

▶ A child with poor coordination, e.g. does not seem to be in control of body movements.

▶ A child who still finds it difficult to walk up and down stairs without adult support.

▶ A child who constantly invades the space of others, e.g. during circle or carpet time, by either sitting too close or standing on other children to get to 'their place'.

Points for Practice

Carefully observe which hand a child has a preference for and, if necessary, make sure you provide left-handed scissors and other tools for those who need them.

Note

All settings should already have a range of left-handed tools as there will always be children who need them.

Hands-on activity

▶ Carry out an audit of your equipment and count how many left-handed pieces of equipment you have.

▶ Check the website www.anythingleft-handed.co.uk for ideas for new equipment. Most educational suppliers also carry a range of left-handed equipment.

Further reading

Casey, Theresa (2007) *Environments for Outdoor Play*. Paul Chapman Publishing.
Doherty, Jonathan and Bailey, Richard (2002) *Supporting Physical Development and Physical Education in the Early Years*, Supporting Early Learning. Open University Press.
Warner, Maureen (2003) *Physical Development*, Foundation Blocks. Brilliant Publications.
Woodfield, Lynda (2004) *Physical Development in the Early Years*, Classmates. Continuum.

CHAPTER SEVEN

Look, listen and note: themed observations

The aim of this chapter is to introduce a range of observational techniques which can support practitioners in identifying additional needs.

It encourages practitioners to focus on the child's areas of strength and those which are causing concern and then to analyse their observations in order to best meet the child's needs.

The chapter sets out:

▶ an overview of observation

▶ themed observations

▶ follow-up sheets for specific areas of child development

and includes:

▶ a Hands-on activity

▶ further reading.

The key to identifying additional needs in young children lies in observation. It is the single most powerful tool that practitioners have in order to gather information and evidence and to pinpoint a child's areas of strength and difficulty.

Once these observations are put together with all the other information we have about a child we can begin to analyse and plan what needs to be done to best support that child. All early years settings have a system in place to observe and record children's progress. This can take the form of notebooks, post-its, photographs, samples of work, etc. Different children are usually observed each week by their key person and this continues on a rolling programme throughout the year.

There are some children, however, for whom more in-depth observation is needed as, for one reason or other, they are causing concern to those who work with them. The process is straightforward but not easy as there is a skill to observation which only comes with practice. All practitioners should have the chance to carry out extended observations to ensure that they develop this important skill.

What is a themed observation?

This type of in-depth observation involves looking at children for a longer period of time, usually up to twenty minutes, and focusing on a particular area.

Unlike a narrative observation, only the area of focus is recorded in the practitioner's notes. For example, if speech and language are the areas of focus, then only what a child says, the noises made and the responses, verbal or non-verbal, are noted down.

If during the observation it becomes apparent that there are other difficulties then further observations need to be carried out in that area.

The diagrams on the following pages will help you to plan these observations.

Using Observations to Help Identify Additional Needs

Establish your area of concern

This is usually straightforward as you will almost certainly have noticed things which have made you wonder or worry about what is happening for an individual child in one or more areas of development. You will already have discussed these concerns with other members of staff and parents and asked for their perspective.

Carry out a 'themed observation'

The observation needs to be carefully planned as you will need to be undisturbed by other children for up to twenty minutes. The support of other staff is essential. You may have to rearrange staff or enlist extra help in order to free yourself from normal duties. In some circumstances it will be necessary to 'set up' a particular game or activity which will provide you with the information that you need. Again this may involve another member of staff working with a group of children so that you can then observe.

Many settings have ways to show children that they should not be disturbed at this time. A badge or hat which indicates that you have 'special work' or 'writing' to do is very useful and children soon get used to this idea.

Analyse your observation using the 'follow-up sheet'

Once you have carried out your observation it is important to analyse it carefully and to reflect upon what you have seen. It is very helpful to have observations carried out by other members of staff as well which can then be discussed together. Having completed the follow-up sheet you should then have a list of significant points.

Consider other factors including developmental expectations

Check out your significant points with any other information you have about the child, including their strengths. This will help you to see your observations in terms of the whole child. You should refer back to the developmental guides to make sure that you have appropriate expectations. Remember, however, these are not set in stone and each child's development may vary.

Decide on a 'plan of action'

The significant points and conclusions you reach, having looked at the observations, should enable you to plan what needs to happen next. This plan should be incorporated into the everyday planning of your setting.

Review progress

After an agreed time the plan should be reviewed to see if it is being effective. More observations should be carried out to provide evidence of progress.

Begin again

For many children this targeted planning will be enough to help them make progress. There will be a minority of children who despite this will need additional support. These children will be discussed more fully in the next chapter.

Themed Observation Sheet

Child's name:	Date:
Focus of observation:	Observed by:

Time	

Themed Observation Follow-up Sheet

What was noticed

What this could tell us

What we should do next

Observed by: Discussed with:

Follow-up sheets

Sometimes it is helpful to have a specific follow-up sheet which will prompt you to ask the right sorts of questions and act as an extra tool to help you analyse your observations.

Speech, language or communication follow-up sheets

The following pages contain:

▶ an information sheet to help practitioners to clarify some of the terminology used when talking about speech, language and communication – this may help practitioners accurately identify any difficulties in what is a very wide area;

▶ some general advice on children who have English as an Additional Language (EAL);

▶ a speech, language and communication follow-up sheet.

Physical development follow-up sheets

Physical development refers not only to how well children are growing and changing but also the development of particular groups of skills. It is important before you carry out an observation to be clear about which area you are focusing on.

The following pages contain

▶ an information sheet to help clarify some of the terminology used when describing physical development – this may help practitioners to identify accurately any difficulties;

▶ a physical development observation follow-up sheet.

Points for Practice

Ask parents if their child has had a hearing check and if in doubt suggest that they request one from their GP or health visitor.

It can be useful when looking at a child's physical development to have some information from parents about when they reached various milestones, e.g. first sat up, crawled, walked, etc.

Some children are more comfortable and/or confident with physical activity and the skills it involves than others. This could be as a result of a lack of experience, a previous accident or injury or even an overprotective parent. As for all other areas, information about these things should be gathered from parents in order to give a complete picture of the child.

You may need to 'set up' various activities in order to observe the skills you are focusing on. For example, an obstacle course or circuit outside can help you to observe fully a child's motor skills. It is fun and all the children can join in.

Jargon Buster

Speech, Language and Communication

Speech refers to using the voice to make sounds. The tongue, lips, teeth and mouth all contribute to forming sounds. These sounds are combined together to form words. Speech difficulties occur when a child has difficulties in producing or combining these sounds. These are sometimes referred to as difficulties with pronunciation or articulation.

Language involves using two different skills:

- *Receptive language* – this is being able to understand what is said to you. This can mean understanding spoken language or non-verbal language such as sign language or Braille, etc.

- *Expressive language* – This means being able to express or convey what you mean to others. This can be done through words, sign language, gestures, facial expression or body language.

Communication means being able to give and receive messages. It can be done with or without words through talking, gesturing, signing, etc. It includes social interaction and how we relate to those around us.

Can children have difficulties in just one of these areas?

Yes, some children might have difficulties with the articulation of words, for example, but have no difficulties in understanding words, expressing themselves or in their social interaction.

Often difficulties are interconnected. For example, children who have difficulties in expressing themselves may find social interaction quite difficult as well.

Who can help if we are concerned about a child's development?

As the name suggests a speech and language therapist is the specialist in this area. Most speech and language therapy services accept referrals from parents and pre-schools (with parental permission).

English as an Additional Language

What if a child's first language is not English?

Research suggests that bilingualism can benefit children's overall academic and intellectual development and progress. So while children who have English as an additional language may need extra support to develop their language skills, this in itself should *not* be regarded as a special need.

> *A child must not be regarded as having a learning difficulty solely because their home language is different from the language in which they will be taught.*
>
> (DfEE, 2001)

It is very important that practitioners not only recognise and value a child's home language but also use the knowledge they already have about language as a starting point for building on and supporting their development of English. The importance of working alongside parents, valuing their contribution and, where necessary, finding ways to communicate with them cannot be stressed enough.

> *Bilingualism is an asset, and the first language has a continuing and significant role in identity, learning and the acquisition of additional languages.*
>
> (DCSF, 2007: 4)

What if you are still concerned?

Sometimes a child has English as an additional language *as well as* a special need. This is sometimes very difficult to assess but if you are concerned about the language development of a bilingual child the starting point should be the same as for any other child.

▶ Gather information about how well the child is developing in their home language/s. It is often the case that if a child is having difficulties in their first or home language they may also then have difficulties in developing English.

▶ Carry out a 'themed observation', 'follow-up sheet' and 'planning and review' cycle.

▶ If there is any doubt about a child's language development, help should be sought from outside professionals such as speech and language therapists. They are often able to arrange for dual language assessments to be carried out.

Speech, Language and Communication Observation Follow-up Sheet
Analysing Your Observation

What was noticed	What this tells us and what we need to do
How? How did they communicate? *e.g.* Was it babbling or clear speech? Did the child use gesture, facial expression, signs? Did they change their tone of voice or pitch? **Who?** To whom did the child speak? With whom did they interact? *e.g.* Practitioner or peer/individual or group? **What?** What did they actually ***say***? *e.g.* Did they use babble, words, phrases, sentences, questions? What did they ***understand***? *e.g.* Did they follow an instruction, answer a question or comply with a request? **Where?** Where did this take place/the context? *e.g.* In the home corner with two other children/outside, etc. **When?** When did they speak? *e.g.* Were they initiating interaction, answering, talking alongside or to themselves? **Why?** What was the purpose of the interaction and were they successful in their aim? *e.g.* Were they trying to join in with another child's play or expressing a need? **If not, why not?** What was the reason the child was unsuccessful in their communication? *e.g.* They were not understood or did not understand, too quiet, did not have the vocabulary, etc.	

Jargon Buster
Physical Development

Gross motor skills

This refers to those skills associated with, as the name suggests, using the large muscles of the body. This includes walking, running and climbing. Gross motor skills develop first with physical coordination and control beginning at a child's head, working downwards through the arms, hands, etc. and finally the legs and feet.

Fine motor skills

Most commonly this refers to smaller movements more associated with dexterity and more precise hand and finger movements. Sometimes called fine manipulative skills, this includes threading, cutting, pencil and brush control, etc.

Also included, however, are gross manipulative skills which refer to movements of a single limb, such as the arm, for example large sweeping movements such as those needed for throwing, catching or turning a skipping rope.

There is evidence to suggest that the development of these gross manipulative skills also helps to develop the finer movements such as those needed later on for writing.

Sensory development

This refers to the development of the five senses: hearing, vision, smell, touch and taste.

Generally children with a significant hearing or visual impairment would be identified before they start at an early years setting, either by a paediatrician or another health professional such as a health visitor.

However, it should be remembered that many young children suffer from repeated colds and coughs or glue ear. This can reduce hearing enough, at this crucial stage of learning, to have an impact, particularly on a child's speech and language development.

Physical Development Observation Follow-up Sheet
Analysing Your Observation

What was noticed	What this tells us and what we need to do
What did the child do? *e.g.* Climbed on the climbing frame, went around the road track, avoided the ropes, cutting and sticking activity.	
What equipment did the child use? *e.g.* Ladder, slide and rope bridge; tricycle, scooter, scissors and glue stick.	
How did they use the equipment? *e.g.* Went up the ladder one rung at a time with right leg leading, held on to the side of the slide not the rungs; pushed themselves along, did not pedal; changed scissor hands frequently, tore the paper rather than cut, could not twist the glue stick up.	
What was the child's attitude to the activity? *e.g.* Very hesitant, constantly looked for help, got very frustrated; reluctant to participate, needed lots of encouragement; could concentrate for 1 minute.	
Was the child's ability within the range of what is developmentally appropriate? *e.g.* Was age appropriate; would have been expected to be more skilled; exceeds expectations.	

Observing behaviour

Observing behaviour is frequently different to other observations because often we cannot plan our observation in the same way as we do others. Children do not always 'perform' just because we are observing them and sometimes we have to record what happened after the event.

It is important, however, that we record the information as if it was a planned observation, as this gives us an opportunity to properly analyse what has happened. The analysis is just as important when observing behaviour as it is for any other focus and the subsequent planning is crucial to affecting change.

Many children's behaviour will, on close examination, form a pattern. Once this pattern is recognised and understood steps can be taken to support the child to make better choices. In many cases changing what happens before and after inappropriate behaviour is what changes the behaviour itself.

Behaviour observations can be recorded on the '**themed observation**' sheets. In this case everything connected to behaviour is focused on and written down in a narrative style. This is then analysed on the '**follow-up**' sheet.

Sometimes, however, it is more helpful to break down the observation into three areas as we write. This is also sometimes called the ABC method:

A – meaning Antecedent or what happened *before* the incident.

B – meaning Behaviour or what the child did *during* the incident.

C – meaning Consequence or what happened *after* the incident.

Breaking down the behaviour in this way helps us to really think about what we have seen. The follow-up sheet helps us to ask ourselves the right sorts of question in order to plan what we need to do and how we can support the child.

On the following pages are examples of the format for recording this type of observation. Both the observation and the follow-up sheets have notes which will help you to complete your own observation.

Blank copies of the record sheet can be found on the CD-ROM.

Points for Practice

Be objective – write down only what you see.

Avoid pre-judging what you will see and jumping to conclusions.

Remember you need at least three or four observations to make your conclusions reliable.

» Ask other members of staff to carry out some of the observations.

» Discuss what you have seen with colleagues who may have a different perspective.

Observing and Recording Behaviour Sheet

Before ~ putting it into context	During ~ recording the actual event	After ~ what happened next
Who? Where? When? And Why?	**What?**	**And then?**
This is when we have the chance to put the behaviour into context. It can be very important when trying to establish whether or not there is a pattern forming.	This part of the observation is when we record what actually happened, e.g. What did the target child do ~ snatched a toy, pinched another child, threw a toy across the room?	We then need to look at what happened next for all those involved.
List details of *who* the target child was with at the time. Is it when a particular member of staff or child is with them? This can often reveal clashes of personality, another child who provokes or even show other children to be displaying equally inappropriate behaviour which we may not have noticed.	Note down what actions or words the target child used or displayed. This is important when we analyse what behaviour we want to change.	What did the *target child* do next? Did they continue playing, did they seem upset, did they run away from the situation?

What did the *other child* involved do? Did they retaliate, did they walk away, did they become upset? |
Where the inappropriate behaviour occurs is another aspect to the observation. Is it always outside on the bikes, in the messy play area or on the carpet?		What did the *surrounding children* do? Did they call for an adult, did they become involved themselves, were they shocked or upset or unaware of what was happening?
Recording *when* a particular child displays inappropriate behaviour can prove very interesting. Is it always at the end of the morning, just before lunch, every Monday morning, when you are settling down for a story or at tidy-up time?		What did the *adults* do? Did they give the target child attention, did they ask for an explanation, did they comfort the other child, did they brush the incident aside?
Why ~ was there a *trigger*? For some children tiredness, hunger, being left first thing in the morning, having to sit for circle time or being asked to tidy up when they are engrossed in a game can be the *trigger* which sets them off.		By considering the consequences for all concerned we are able, in the follow-up analysis, to see what might have been a better outcome for all concerned.

Recognising and Planning for Special Needs in the Early Years, SAGE © Chris Dukes and Maggie Smith, 2009

Observing and Recording Behaviour Follow-up Sheet

Analysing Your Observation

How could I have changed what happened before? How could I have prevented the trigger?	What behaviour do I want to change? What behaviour do I want to see instead?	What would have been a better consequence? What would I like to have happened instead?	What do I need to do now?
Look at the context in which the behaviour took place. Then you need to decide if there is anything that you could have changed to prevent the behaviour happening in the first place. If you have more than one observation you might see a pattern beginning to emerge. Sometimes there may be a very clear trigger for a particular behaviour. When you understand what this trigger is or can begin to see why a child behaved in a certain way you are halfway, to being able to support the child to change that behaviour.	It is usually easy to identify unacceptable behaviour. What you need to think about next is what you would prefer the child to do, given the same set of circumstances. It is important to have a very clear idea of what this is because you will need to have a plan to support the child to be able to make better choices in the future.	This involves you looking at what happened after the behaviour occurred and considering the actions of all those involved. It may be that on reflection the staff could have done something different which might have changed the outcome. Perhaps other children in the setting need some support or guidance as well as the target child.	Many settings will use either an Individual Education Plan or a Behaviour Support Plan. These record the target behaviours and the strategies which will be used to support a child.

Recognising and Planning for Special Needs in the Early Years, SAGE © Chris Dukes and Maggie Smith, 2009

✋ Hands-on activity

With parental permission, video some children at your setting.

In a team meeting watch the video/s and fill out the observation sheets above.

Discuss your observations and in pairs draw up an observation follow-up sheet.

📖 Further reading

Department for Children, Schools and Families (2007) *Supporting Children Learning English as an Additional Language: Guidance for Practitioners in the Early Years Foundation Stage.* DCFS.

Department for Education and Employment (2001) *Special Educational needs: Code of Practice.* DfEE.

Drury, R. (2006) *Young Bilingual Children learning at Home and School.* Trentham Books.

Mathieson, Kay (2007) *Identifying Special Needs in the Early Years.* Paul Chapman Publishing.

CHAPTER EIGHT

Next steps: plan, do, review

The aim of this chapter is to help practitioners plan the next steps to support a child when, despite all previously described discussion, observation, support and strategies, a child still does not make the progress that might be expected.

It gives advice on how to work in partnership with parents and other professionals to address a child's needs.

The chapter sets out:

▶ a definition of special educational needs and working with the Code of Practice for Special Educational Needs

▶ the role of the early years special needs or inclusion coordinator

▶ writing and reviewing individual education plans

▶ working with parents

▶ child participation

▶ individual education plans and planning

▶ referrals and seeking additional advice

and includes:

▶ a Hands-on activity

▶ further reading.

What next?

Some children will not make the progress we had hoped for or expected even when staff have:

▶ investigated the child's individual circumstances;

▶ talked with parents and colleagues;

▶ considered their age and stage of development;

▶ reflected upon the environment;

▶ carried out themed observations;

▶ planned and differentiated activities;

▶ tried a variety of strategies.

These children will need more targeted support and perhaps additional advice from outside professionals. At this stage they could be described as having special or additional needs.

The practices and procedures which should now be followed are laid down in the **Special Educational Needs: Code of Practice (DfEE, 2001). Chapter 4** of the Code is specific to early years settings and is summarised in the following pages.

The key to what follows is the necessity to make plans and provisions which are **additional to** or **different from** those which are made for most other children.

The children concerned are currently described as having **special educational needs,** or **learning difficulties** or **disabilities**.

The role of the Special Needs or Inclusion Coordinator

Once a child has been identified as having special or additional needs the **Special Needs Inclusion Coordinator** (SENCO) of a setting would be expected to take the lead. This might involve further assessing a child's needs and ensuring that appropriate steps are taken to meet those needs.

They would also, in liaison with colleagues, parents and professionals, plan, record, monitor and review any action that is taken.

The Code of Practice explains that the SENCO should have responsibility for:

▶ ensuring liaison with parents and other professionals in respect of children with special educational needs;

▶ advising and supporting other practitioners in the setting;

▶ ensuring that appropriate individual education plans are in place;

▶ ensuring that relevant background information about individual children with special educational needs is collected, recorded and updated.

The Code of Practice sets out very clearly the procedures to be followed once a child is identified as having special or additional needs. The importance of both parental involvement and child participation is a key principle in this process.

The actions which follow are called a **graduated response** and are described on page 94.

The Graduated Response

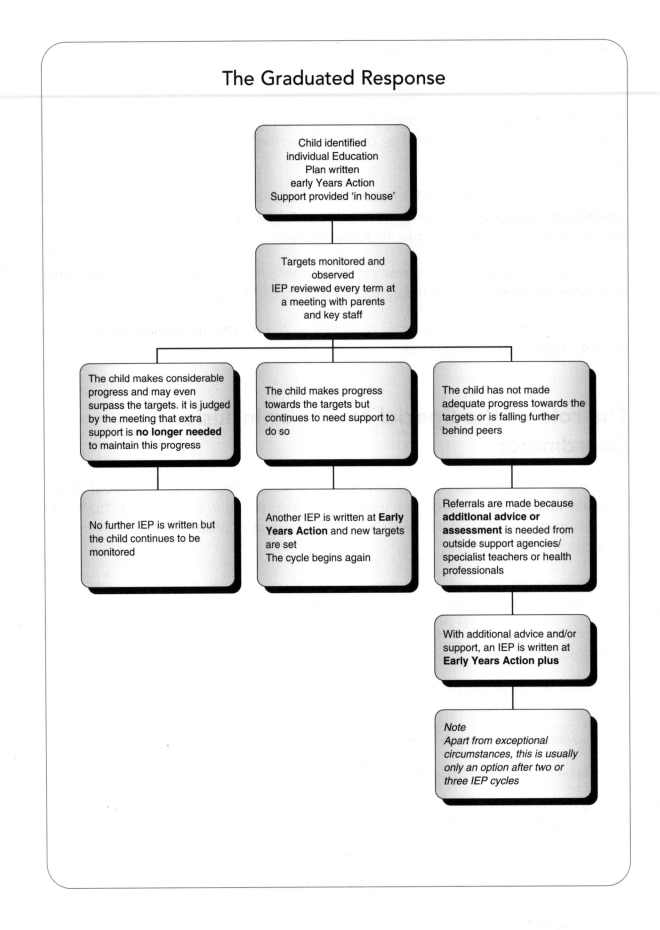

Child identified
individual Education
Plan written
early Years Action
Support provided 'in house'

↓

Targets monitored and
observed
IEP reviewed every term at
a meeting with parents
and key staff

The child makes considerable
progress and may even
surpass the targets. it is judged
by the meeting that extra
support is **no longer needed**
to maintain this progress

The child makes progress
towards the targets but
continues to need support to
do so

The child has not made
adequate progress towards the
targets or is falling further
behind peers

No further IEP is written but
the child continues to be
monitored

Another IEP is written at **Early
Years Action** and new targets
are set
The cycle begins again

Referrals are made because
**additional advice or
assessment** is needed from
outside support agencies/
specialist teachers or health
professionals

With additional advice and/or
support, an IEP is written at
Early Years Action plus

---

*Note
Apart from exceptional
circumstances, this is usually
only an option after two or
three IEP cycles*

Recognising and Planning for Special Needs in the Early Years, SAGE © Chris Dukes and Maggie Smith, 2009

The graduated response explained

Early Years Action

▶ The identified child is said to be at *Early Years Action*.

▶ This involves a cycle of observing, planning and reviewing in a similar way to the individualised planning expected for all children.

▶ In the case of a child with special educational needs, learning difficulty or disability the planning tool is called an *individual education plan (IEP)* or an *individual plan (IP)*.

▶ The Code also makes it clear that the key person 'should remain responsible for working with the child on a daily basis and for planning and delivering an individualised programme' (DfES, 2001, page 34).

▶ The IEP is written at a meeting which the SENCO, key person, parents and anyone else involved attends. This should be organised by the SENCO.

▶ As a result of the individual education plan support which is considered 'additional' or 'different' to that which would be given to all children is provided for the child. All intervention or support is carried out 'in house', usually by the key person, as part of the everyday planning and provision in the setting.

▶ The child's progress towards the IEP targets is reviewed, usually termly, at a *review meeting* which parents, key person and SENCO attend. Again this is organised by the setting SENCO.

▶ The various outcomes of this review meeting are detailed on the diagram opposite which lays out the graduated response.

If a child still makes inadequate progress despite additional support, one outcome may be that a child moves on to *Early Years Action Plus*.

Early Years Action Plus

Children at Early Years Action Plus are subject to the same IEP planning and review cycle as those at Early Years Action. The main difference is that there are often more professionals involved. These may include speech and language therapists, physiotherapists, etc.

These professionals should be invited to IEP meetings and asked for reports and suggestions for targets for the child. A note should be made on the individual education plan of any contributions made by a professional to show that you as a setting are listening to specialist advice.

Keeping track of all those who need to be invited can be quite a task so it is useful to keep a record for your own benefit.

Statutory assessment

There is a small minority of children whose needs are deemed to be severe, complex and life-long. Again, after two or three IEP cycles at Early Years Action Plus, these children may well need to go through the *statutory assessment* procedure or request such an assessment.

There are clear guidelines in the Code of Practice about how this is to be carried out and local authorities have to meet various standards and timescales. They also have a duty to provide support for parents through parent partnership groups. Information and advice on this process should be sought through local agencies.

Individual Education Plan

INDIVIDUAL EDUCATION PLAN No......	EYA/EYA + /ST
Child's name:	D.o.B.:

Targets set Date:	Review Date:
Target 1: Action/Strategies By whom	Achieved? What has/has not been successful?
Target 2: Action/Strategies/Resources By whom	Achieved? What has/has not been successful?
Target 3: Action/Strategies/Resources By whom	Achieved? What has/has not been successful?

IEP REVIEW

Child's strengths:

Parent/Child's comments:

Additional/New information:

New IEP needed?   Yes/No Change in Code of Practice?   Yes/No

Further steps/Action:

Those involved in writing/reviewing IEP (including reports/advice) or needing copies:

New IEP written   Yes/No
Date of next IEP review:
Name of person completing this form: Position:

Setting targets and writing individual education plans

Setting targets is not as easy as it sounds! Time should be taken to think about these carefully and it is often better to have some ideas in mind before you have the planning meeting. Practitioners should concentrate on specific tasks, the child's success should be measurable and resources and strategies should be made explicit. In this way progress is easy to assess.

Good targets are often referred to as being **SMART**:

S – Specific

M – Measurable

A – Achievable

R – Realistic

T – Time bound

For example, if you would like a child *to be able to share and play with other children* the target may be:

> ▶ To play a turn-taking game
>
> ▶ With one other child and the key person
>
> ▶ For 10 minutes each day
>
> ▶ Using the shopping and bus stop games
>
> ▶ The person taking the turn will wear a hat.

The targets set out on an IEP are obviously not the only aspects which will be worked on with the child but are a measure of a particular skill it is hoped to improve.

> For example, if you would like a child to be able to *develop their fine motor skills* the target may be:
>
> ▶ To be able to thread 5 small beads onto a string
>
> While this would be your measure of achievement to see if the child had improved it is not the only activity you would practise in order to develop the skills!
>
> A whole variety of fine motor activities could be provided including the specific bead threading so that these skills could be developed.

Reviewing individual education plans

A *review meeting* is an integral part of the IEP process and is held after an agreed period, usually a term or three months. The key person, pre-school setting SENCO and parents should all attend and the child's progress towards the targets is discussed. The review meeting is also an opportunity for both setting and parents to update information and pass on any new developments. Practitioners may find it helpful to do some observations of the child before the meeting so they have the latest report on the child's progress. It should be a positive meeting and one which celebrates what the child has achieved.

Each IEP target should be looked at in turn and an evaluation made as to whether or not the child has reached the target. It is helpful to note any particular strategies or resources that have been successful and those which have not really worked. In this way a picture emerges of how best to support a child which is a useful record for future planning.

Where a child does not achieve their targets it is always worth considering if they were realistic and achievable within the time frame (**SMART**) before deciding on revised or new targets.

Child participation

It is always important to consider the views of a child when planning and reviewing, not only individual education plans and targets, but also methods of support. With very young children or those who have limited communication skills this can be a challenge.

▶ Children will often find it easier to express themselves through drawing and this can be a way forward in trying to collect together their thoughts and feelings on to paper.

▶ Carefully managed '*conferencing*' is another way of a familiar adult talking to children to find out what they are thinking and how they are feeling. By asking the right sorts of questions staff can give children an opportunity to express what they like, what they find difficult and how they like to play or learn.

▶ More general questioning can provide a profile of a child's likes, dislikes, friends, special people, favourite activities and what makes them upset or happy. Where a child has an IEP it can be helpful to focus the questions around the targets.

IEPs and working with parents

Working in partnership with parents is essential. Many parents are unfamiliar with IEPs so it is important for practitioners to help them understand the purpose of an IEP or IP and how they can be involved in it.

The 'Let's Talk About ... Individual Education Plans' sheet on page 103 can be given as a quick guide for parents and is also a useful summary for practitioners.

Sample Individual Education Plan

INDIVIDUAL EDUCATION PLAN No.1	EYA / EYA+ / ST
Child's name: Kate Smiles	**D.o.B.**: 6.6.05

Targets set Date: October '07	**Review** Date: January '08
Target 1: Kate will retell a simple story using picture clues **Action/Strategies**: Share a simple story with Kate pointing at the pictures as you speak then ask Kate to read it to you, or her teddy or another child. **By whom**: The same book will be used both at home and at pre-school. Kate will select a book and take it back and forward between pre-school and home for up to a week.	**Achieved?** Yes **What has/has not been successful?** Kate has been working hard on this target by looking at a simple story book a week both at home and at pre-school.
Target 2: Kate will complete a 6-piece inset puzzle independently **Action/Strategies/Resources**: Kate will take home a variety of fine motor activities at the weekend from pre-school. These will be some of the activities she has tried at pre-school. **By whom**: Key worker Sarah and Kate's parents. Coordinated by SENCO.	**Achieved?** Needs to be consolidated **What has/has not been successful?** Kate sometimes finds puzzles frustrating as she only likes to use the type of puzzle with a handle. These have been hard to find.
Target 3: Kate will put on her outdoor shoes and coat by herself when going outside (weather permitting) **Action/Strategies/Resources:** All staff will support Kate to use the method she uses at home to put her coat on. Kate will be given extra time to put her coat on and a chair to sit on when putting her shoes on. Staff will ensure her shoes are on the right feet. **By whom:** All setting staff and at home with parents.	**Achieved?** Yes **What has/has not been successful?** Kate has loved showing her friends her technique for putting her coat on. All the children are now using this method. Kate finds her slip-on shoes easy but her shoes with the buckle are more difficult and staff support her when she wears these.

The most obvious way to get parents involved is through the targets and activities themselves. Joint target-setting can strengthen relationships between parent and practitioner as well as proving hugely beneficial to the child.

With their expert knowledge of their child parents have much to contribute to planning these targets. Practitioners need to recognise and listen to parents' suggestions and ideas and consider them alongside their own experience of the child, the setting and the curriculum.

Where joint targets are set for working on at home as well as at the pre-school, consideration should be given to targets which are:

▶ set within the context of everyday play and experiences at home;

▶ are not laboured, overdone or regarded as a chore;

▶ have variety and fun built in;

▶ take into account the interests of the child;

▶ are realistic in terms of what a parent is able to do in their individual circumstances, e.g. time, equipment;

▶ do not make parents or their child feel pressurised.

Points for Practice

Some parents will feel more comfortable with the idea of joint targets than others for a variety of reasons. Practitioners should be sensitive to this and follow a few general rules:

▶ Avoid using jargon.

▶ Illustrate what you mean by giving a few examples of how a target could be worked on at home.

▶ Ask if parents have the toy, game or equipment needed.

▶ Offer to lend equipment or toys.

▶ Plan an opportunity for you to model a particular strategy while parents observe.

▶ Allow time for parents to ask questions and clarify any issues.

▶ Check how things are going after a week or so in case parents need further support.

Let's Talk About...

Individual Plans (IPs) or Individual Education Plans (IEPs)

Q. What is an Individual Plan or Individual Education Plan?

A. These are both types of plan written for individual children who may have additional needs in order to help them make progress. The plan will:

- record basic information about the child;

- record their strengths and the things that motivate them;

- record the areas in which they need some help;

- set specific targets for the child to work towards;

- detail the support, resources and strategies which will be used to help them achieve those targets;

- be reviewed regularly (usually once a term) to see what progress has been made and to set new targets.

Q. Who decides which targets should be set?

A. The targets will be set during discussions at an IP or IEP meeting which is usually held at the early years setting. You as parents, as well as practitioners and anybody working with your child such as speech therapists or physiotherapists, will be asked to suggest suitable targets.

Q. Are these targets the only thing your child will be working on at nursery?

A. Your child will be doing all the usual nursery activities and the targets will be incorporated into the nursery planning. Sometimes it may be appropriate for some individual or small-group time to be allocated when staff can work more specifically on targets with your child.

Q. How will I be involved?

A. You can be involved by:
- working on and practising the targets at home;

- attending the IP or IEP meetings;

- giving your views on how your child is progressing towards their targets;

- making suggestions for what they may need to work on next;

- liaising with the professionals involved with your child to make sure they contribute and give advice as well.

Recognising and Planning for Special Needs in the Early Years, SAGE © Chris Dukes and Maggie Smith, 2009

Writing Individual Education Plans
The Planning Cylce

Use all available information including observations to identify two or three targets for a child to work towards.

Specify the strategies, resources and staff needed to support the child in meeting the targets.

Writing Individual Education Plans - The Planning Cylce

Set new targets. Work from the Child's strengths and interests wherever possible.

Involve parents by planning joint targets which can be worked on at home. Share strategies and resources.

Review the IEP termly.
Note down any successes and strategies or activities which haven't worked so well.

Monitor progress regularly. Carry out observations to evidence this.

IEPs and pre-school planning

Every pre-school will have its own way of planning both for the short and longer term. It is important that any planning for children with special or additional needs is incorporated into the usual planning rather than being seen as something separate. While individual children may have particular targets they should as far as possible be worked towards during the normal course of the day.

IEPs and Planning – 20 Points for Practice

- IEPs are **confidential** documents and should not be on general display.
- Keep copies of IEPs in your **planning file** or somewhere readily available to staff. IEPs should be a working document that all practitioners feel they can change, add to, make notes on and use for the benefit of the child.
- Refer to the targets, activities and strategies on the IEPs when you think about the **activities** you are planning for the whole group or setting.
- Consider a child's learning style when thinking about how to present an activity.
- Check that your setting has the **equipment** for any activities suggested on IEPs.
- Make sure that you allow **time** for a staff member to work with a child or group of children.
- Keep **all staff** up to date with a child's targets, as working on IEP targets is the responsibility of everybody in a room or setting.
- Highlight on your planning sheet **when** a target activity is being carried out and **by whom**.
- Decide who will be responsible for **monitoring** that the child is being supported to reach their targets.
- Build **extra observations** into your observation schedule for children with individual education plans.
- Try to **record** how a child is progressing towards their targets on a weekly basis. This helps when it comes to reviewing IEPs.
- Note down when a child reaches or surpasses a target and **extend** the target if necessary.
- Be **flexible** about reviewing IEPs, particularly those connected to behaviour targets, as these may need to be reviewed more often and plans and strategies adjusted.
- If delivering particular programmes such as exercises suggested by physiotherapists, ensure these are broken down into **manageable** sessions that work for your setting.
- Make sure that advisers or professionals have **realistic** expectations of what you can manage in your setting.
- Encourage parents to contribute by having **home–pre-school targets**.
- **Liaise with parents** about joint targets. Communication books or diaries are one way of doing this.
- **Sharing** equipment, toys, games or books with parents is a good way of reinforcing skills and learning.
- Try to **involve children** in planning some of their activities and work from their strengths and preferences.
- Remember that though they are important, IEP targets are a way of **measuring** progress and are only a small part of what a child will be offered during a day at a pre-school.

 Recognising and Planning for Special Needs in the Early Years, SAGE © Chris Dukes and Maggie Smith, 2009

Referrals and seeking additional advice

For those children who, even with more targeted support, still do not make the progress we would expect or hope for, additional advice often needs to be obtained from professionals with more specialist knowledge.

Every local authority will have a range of advisors from early years, education and health services and these are accessed differently in each authority.

There is an increasing move towards a more seamless and coherent support for children with special needs and their families. There is recognition of the need to bring both health and education services together and create coordinated provision.

> Remember: parental permission must be obtained before any discussion with a professional outside your pre-school.

Communicating with other professionals

It is very important to try to liaise with any professional who works with a child in your pre-school. Children's needs are often slightly different in a pre-school setting than they might be at home and practitioners sometimes have different questions and queries from parents regarding individual children.

The expertise that a particular professional has can help provide you with specific and focused IEP targets and their ideas and suggestions can feed into your planning for the child.

Communicating with professionals from outside your own pre-school can be of huge benefit to the child but it can also be a frustrating and time-consuming task for you to reach the person you need when you need them. Most professionals welcome dialogue with practitioners and difficulties in communicating are largely due to the heavy work and case loads which most professionals have, rather than any unwillingness to share information.

Jargon Buster
Who's Who in Education

Curriculum advisers

These are teachers who can give advice and support on curriculum and planning issues. They will advise on general good practice throughout the pre-school.

Inclusion adviser/area SENCO

These are teachers or early years specialists who can advise on inclusion and working with children with special needs. They often have extensive experience or specialist qualifications in working with children with particular needs, such as hearing or visual impairments. Some are involved in direct teaching while others fulfil a more advisory role.

Portage worker

Portage is a home teaching service. It works with children who have special needs aged 0–5 years and their families. Portage workers visit children in their homes on a regular basis to assess and teach new skills. They model the teaching of each skill to enable parents and carers to work with their child in between visits. In this way parents and workers are able to work together, pool their knowledge of the child and support each other. Many authorities have portage workers or those who carry out a similar role.

Educational psychologist

An educational psychologist provides specialist assessment of all kinds of learning difficulties. They can give advice on teaching and management strategies and behaviour management. They will always become involved if a child is having a statutory assessment.

The Pre-school Learning Alliance

The workers are experienced practitioners with a wide range of knowledge and expertise who can help, support and advise on a variety of issues.

Jargon Buster
Who's Who in Health

Clinical psychologist

Clinical psychologists work within health service settings. They provide individual and family counselling, family therapy and advice. They can advise and support on a variety of issues including behaviour management and conditions such as autism.

Speech and language therapist

Speech and language therapists will assess, give advice to families and work directly with children who have a speech, language or communication disorder. They also work with children who have related eating and swallowing difficulties, giving advice on feeding, sucking, food, and mouth and tongue movement.

Physiotherapist

Physiotherapists work mainly with children with physical difficulties or delay. They give advice and support and plan individual programmes which centre on issues such as exercise, coordination and balance. They will also advise on specialist equipment like splints, braces, wheelchairs and buggies.

Occupational therapist

Occupational therapists work with children who need help in developing practical life skills because of some form of physical, psychological or social delay or disability. They provide advice and access to specialised equipment both at home and in the pre-school, such as chairs, bathing or toileting aids and adaptations to everyday items.

Community doctors and paediatricians

Doctors and paediatricians work alongside parents to identify and diagnose various illnesses or conditions. They monitor medical conditions as the child grows older and can also refer to other health service professionals.

Health visitors

Every pre-school child has a health visitor allocated through their local GP. Health visitors will visit families at home when a child is born and also run various clinics for immunisations, sleep and general development checks. They are available for help, support and advice on all development and health issues.

Social workers

Social workers support children and families in difficult circumstances. They can provide advice and access to other social services provision such as respite care. They will also become involved when there are child protection issues or procedures in place.

 Recognising and Planning for Special Needs in the Early Years, SAGE © Chris Dukes and Maggie Smith, 2009

Getting the Most Out of Talking to Outside Professionals

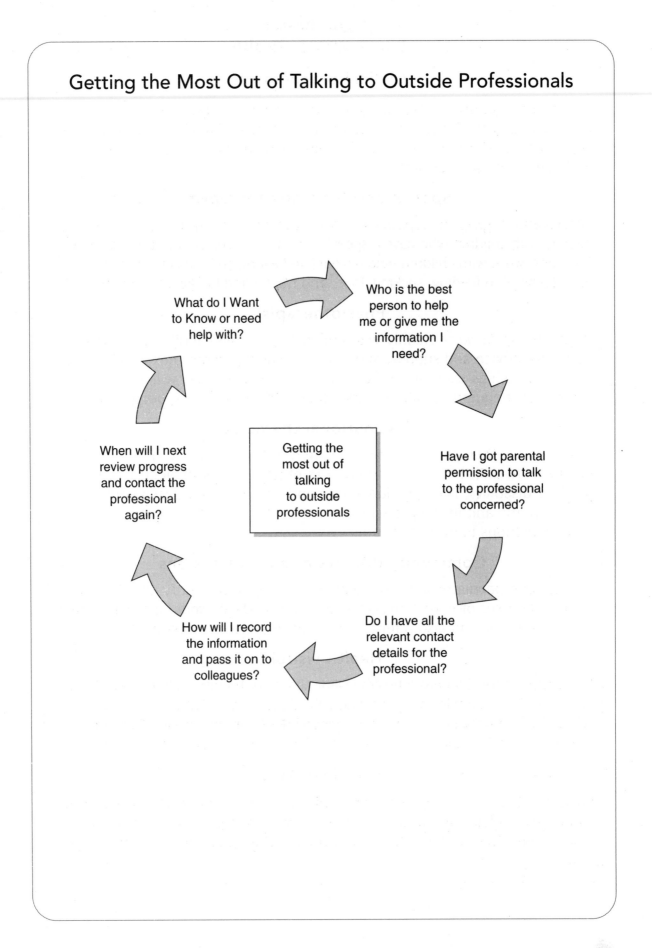

Getting the most out of talking to outside professionals

What do I Want to Know or need help with?

Who is the best person to help me or give me the information I need?

Have I got parental permission to talk to the professional concerned?

Do I have all the relevant contact details for the professional?

How will I record the information and pass it on to colleagues?

When will I next review progress and contact the professional again?

Top Tips for Communicating with Professionals

- Remember that any discussions with outside professionals must be done with the knowledge and consent of parents.

- If you have a regular group of professionals who work with your setting make sure that they are introduced on your notice board and in your prospectus.

- Ask parents to help you compile a list of all the professionals involved with their child.

- List their contact details – this makes it easier when arranging meetings and sending letters.

- List days and working hours so you don't waste time ringing on a day they are not at work.

- Ask them their preferred method of communication – e-mails are often convenient for quick enquiries if the person is office based.

- Prepare a list of questions or information you would like before you speak to them. This will help to keep the conversation focused and ensure that you don't forget the point of your call.

- Give at least 4–6 weeks' notice of any meeting you would like them to attend.

- Ask for some written feedback or suggestions for IEP targets if they are unable to attend your meeting.

- Send copies of any relevant documents, such as IEPs, to them to keep them informed of what is happening. This also encourages them to do the same.

- Ask to be put on the circulation list for reports, etc. Make sure parents are in agreement with this.

- Keep a record of all contacts, including telephone calls and e-mails, with a brief note of what was discussed.

- Look at the record before you make your next contact to remind you of what was discussed last time.

- Try to make contact on a regular basis even if it's just to get an update on progress. This helps to build firmer relationships.

- Don't forget to tell parents and colleagues that you have been in touch with an outside professional and let them know what you discussed.

 Recognising and Planning for Special Needs in the Early Years, SAGE © Chris Dukes and Maggie Smith, 2009

Other planning tools you may encounter

Health care plans

Many children at pre-school will have short-term medical needs such as finishing a course of antibiotics or particular needs at a specific time such as an allergic reaction or hay fever. A smaller group will have long-term medical needs to keep them healthy and these children will need a *health care plan*.

For children under five the responsibility for drawing up such a plan lies with a health professional. Many authorities or health care trusts delegate this to health visitors or practice nurses who draw up the plan in conjunction with parents and a pre-school representative.

The plan details the nature of the need, instructions on medication or other actions and if necessary will have a step-by-step emergency plan. It is very important that a health care plan is in place *before* a child starts at your setting, particularly if their needs are serious or life-threatening.

While some children with medical or health needs will also have special educational needs, it should be remembered, however, that 'a medical diagnosis or a disability does not *necessarily* imply a special educational need. It is the child's educational needs rather than a medical diagnosis that must be considered' (see the SEN Code of Practice: DfES, 2001: paras 7:64–7: 67).

Early Support

For children who have complex special needs the Early Support initiative aims to develop a service which involves health, education, social services and voluntary sector organisations working in partnership to provide multi-agency support for children under five and their families.

A model of support and a range of materials have been developed to implement this initiative and health or education professionals working with children with complex needs and their families will have access to these materials.

The Common Assessment Framework

The Common Assessment Framework is designed for children who have additional needs involving more than one service and who require extra support to help them achieve the five *Every Child Matters* outcomes. Most children therefore will not need a CAF.

The CAF is a shared assessment tool which can be used across all children's services in all local areas of England. It has been introduced with the aim of helping early identification of need and to aid planning for and promoting coordinated provision of services.

Again there is a lead professional who coordinates the process and a central contact point where other professionals can establish if a child already has a CAF. The implementation of the CAF varies from authority to authority but the format and process is uniform.

For further information see **www.ecm.gov.uk/caf**.

Hands-on activity

▶ Set up a directory of your local health and education services (as outlined above).

▶ Make contact with some of those professionals and consider inviting them to meet your staff.

Further reading

Department for Education and Science (2005) *Managing Medicines in Schools and Early Years Settings*. DfES.

Drifte, Collette (2005) *A Manual for the Early Years SENCO*. Paul Chapman Publishing.

Dukes, Chris and Smith, Maggie (2006) *A Practical Guide to Pre-School Inclusion*, Hands On Guides. Paul Chapman Publishing.

Dukes, Chris and Smith, Maggie (2007) *Working with Parents of Children with Special Educational Needs*, Hands On Guides. Paul Chapman Publishing.

Wall, Kate (2006) *Special Needs and Early Years*. Paul Chapman Publishing.

Contacts and Useful Organisations

Chris Dukes and Maggie Smith (authors of Hands On Guides)

www.earlymatters.co.uk

BT Education Programme – 'The Better World Campaign' free resources

www.bt.co./education

Department for Children, Schools and Families

www.direct.gov.uk

ICAN

www.ican.org.uk

National Literacy Trust

www.literacytrust.co.uk

National Refugee Integration Forum

www.nrif.org.uk

SureStart

www.surestart.gov.uk

Bibliography

Casey, Theresa (2007) *Environments for Outdoor Play*. Paul Chapman Publishing.

Department for Children, Schools and Families (2007) *Supporting Children Learning English as an Additional Language: Guidance for Practitioners in the Early Years Foundation Stage*. DCFS.

Department for Education and Employment (2001) *Special Educational Needs: Code of Practice*. DfEE.

Department for Education and Science (2005) *Managing Medicines in Schools and Early Years Settings*. DfES.

Department for Education and Skills (2007) *Statutory Framework for the Early Years Foundation Stage*. DfES.

Department for Education and Skills (2008) *Practice Guidance for the Early Years Foundation Stage*. DfES.

Doherty, Jonathan and Bailey, Richard (2002) *Supporting Physical Development and Physical Education in the Early Years*, Supporting Early Learning. Open University Press.

Dowling, Marion (2005) *Young Children's Personal, Social and Emotional Development*, 2nd edn. Paul Chapman Publishing.

Drifte, Collette (2005) *A Manual for the Early Years SENCO*. Paul Chapman Publishing.

Drury, Rose (2006) *Young Bilingual Children Learning at Home and School*. Trentham Books.

Dukes, Chris and Smith, Maggie (2006) *A Practical Guide to Pre-School Inclusion*, Hands On Guides, 2nd edn. Paul Chapman Publishing.

Dukes, Chris and Smith, Maggie (2007) *Developing Pre-school Communication and Language*, Hands On Guides. Paul Chapman Publishing.

Dukes, Chris and Smith, Maggie (2007) *Working with Parents of Children with Special Educational Needs*, Hands On Guides. Paul Chapman Publishing.

Mathieson, Kay (2007) *Identifying Special Needs in the Early Years*. Paul Chapman Publishing.

Meggit, Carolyn (2006) Child Development: *An Illustrated Guide*, 2nd edn. Heinemann.

Miller, Linda, Cable, Carrie and Devereux, Jane (2005) *Developing Early Years Practice*, Foundation Degree Texts. David Fulton Publishers.

National Children's Bureau Enterprise Ltd (2003) *Early Years and the Disability Discrimination Act 1995: What Service Providers Need to Know*. NCB.

Paige-Smith, Alice and Craft, Anna (2007) *Developing Reflective Practice in the Early Years*. Open University Press.

Roberts, Rosemary (2006) *Self-Esteem and Early Learning: Key People from Birth to school*, Zero to Eight Series, 3rd edn. Paul Chapman Publishing.

Sharp, Elizabeth (2005) *Learning Through Talk in the Early Years: Practical Activities for the Classroom*. Paul Chapman Publishing.

Stocks, Sara (2002) *Personal, Social and Emotional Development (What Learning Looks Like ...)*, 2nd revised edn. Step Forward Publishing.

Visser, Jo (2007) *Supporting Personal, Social and Emotional Development*, Everything Early Years How To ... Series. Everything Early Years.

Wall, Kate (2006) *Special Needs and Early Years*. Paul Chapman Publishing.

Warner, Maureen (2003) *Physical Development*, Foundation Blocks. Brilliant Publications.

Woodfield, Lynda (2004) *Physical Development in the Early Years*, Classmates. Continuum.

Index

A Practical Guide to Pre-school Inclusion

About the authors

Chris Dukes is a qualified teacher with over 20 years experience. She has worked in various London Primary schools as a class teacher and later as a member of the Senior Management Team. Chris has a Masters degree in Special Needs and through her later role as a SENCO and support teacher, many years experience of working with children with a variety of needs. Chris has worked closely with staff teams, mentoring, advising and supervising work with children with additional needs, as well as with other education and health professionals. Chris currently works as an Area SENCO supporting Special Needs Co-ordinators and managers in a wide range of pre-school settings. As well as advising she writes courses, delivers training and produces publications.

Maggie Smith began her career as a Nursery Teacher in Birmingham. She has worked as a Peripatetic teacher for an under 5s EAL Team and went on to become the Foundation Stage manager of an Early Years Unit in Inner London. Maggie helped to set up an innovative unit for young children with behavioural difficulties and has also worked supporting families of children with special needs. Maggie has taught on Early Years BTEC and CACHE courses at a college of Higher Education. Maggie currently works as an Area SENCO supporting Special Needs Co-ordinators and managers in a wide range of pre-scool settings. As well as advising she also writes courses, delivers training and produces publications.